Mulholland Drive

Beloved by film and art aficionados and fans of neo-noir cinema *Mulholland Drive* is one of the most important and enigmatic films of recent years. It occupies a central and controversial position in the work of its director, David Lynch, who won the best director award at the 2001 Cannes Film Festival for the movie.

Mulholland Drive in the Routledge *Philosophers on Film* series is the first full philosophical appraisal of Lynch's film. Beginning with an introduction by the editor, the volume explores the philosophical significance of Lynch's film. It discusses the following topics:

- the identity of the self and its persistence through time
- the central, dual roles played by fantasy and reality throughout the film
- whether *Mulholland Drive* is best understood epistemologically via reason and language, or whether, as Lynch himself argues, by one's "inner feelings" and emotions
- parallels between *Mulholland Drive* and Kafka's *The Castle*, both of which put their protagonists at the mercy of unseen forces
- *Mulholland Drive* and romanticism.

Additional key themes are also explored, such as the interpenetration of ethics, classical tragedy, and *Mulholland Drive*, and the contrasting philosophical arguments of Plato and Nietzsche on tragic drama. These themes make *Mulholland Drive* essential and engaging reading for students of philosophy, especially aesthetics and ethics, as well as film studies.

Contributors: A. E. Denham, Zina Giannopoulou, Patrick Lee Miller, Alan Nelson, Robert Sinnerbrink, and F. D. Worrell

Zina Giannopoulou is Associate Professor of Classics at the University of California, Irvine, USA. She is the author of *Plato's Theaetetus as a Second Apology* (2013).

Philosophers on Film

In recent years, the use of film in teaching and doing philosophy has moved to centre stage. Film is increasingly used to introduce key topics and problems in philosophy, from ethics and aesthetics to epistemology, metaphysics and philosophy of mind. It is also acknowledged that some films raise important philosophical questions of their own. Yet until now, dependable resources for teachers and students of philosophy using film have remained very limited. *Philosophers on Film* answers this growing need and is the first series of its kind.

Each volume assembles a team of international contributors to explore a single film in depth, making the series ideal for classroom use. Beginning with an introduction by the editor, each specially-commissioned chapter will discuss a key aspect of the film in question. Additional features include a biography of the director and suggestions for further reading.

Philosophers on Film is an ideal series for students studying philosophy and film, aesthetics, and ethics and anyone interested in the philosophical dimensions of cinema.

- *Talk to Her*, edited by A. W. Eaton
- *The Thin Red Line*, edited by David Davies
- *Memento*, edited by Andre Kania
- *Eternal Sunshine of the Spotless Mind*, edited by Christopher Grau
- *Fight Club*, edited by Thomas Wartenberg
- *Vertigo*, edited by Katalin Makkai
- *Blade Runner*, edited by Amy Coplan
- *Mulholland Drive*, edited by Zina Giannopoulou

Mulholland Drive

Edited by

Zina Giannopoulou

Routledge
Taylor & Francis Group

LONDON AND NEW YORK

First published 2013
by Routledge
2 Park Square, Milton Park, Abingdon, Oxon OX14 4RN

Simultaneously published in the USA and Canada
by Routledge
711 Third Avenue, New York, NY 10017

Routledge is an imprint of the Taylor & Francis Group, an informa business

British Library Cataloguing in Publication Data
A catalogue record for this book is available from the British Library

Library of Congress Cataloging in Publication Data
Mulholland Drive/edited by Zina Giannopoulou.
pages cm
Includes bibliographical references and index.
1. Mulholland Drive (Motion picture) 2. Philosophy in motion
pictures. I. Giannopoulou, Zina, editor of compilation.
PN1997.2.M66M85 2013
791.43'684—dc23
2013011491

ISBN: 978-0-415-82465-1 (hbk)
ISBN: 978-0-415-82466-8 (pbk)
ISBN: 978-0-203-37035-3 (ebk)

Typeset in Joanna
by Florence Production Ltd, Stoodleigh, Devon, UK

Printed and bound by CPI Group (UK) Ltd, Croydon, CR0 4YY

Contents

Notes on contributors

A. E. Denham is a Senior Research Fellow at St Anne's College, Oxford, and is jointly appointed to the Departments of Philosophy and Political Economy at Tulane University, USA. Her research addresses topics in ethics, aesthetics, and the philosophy of mind. She is the author of an interdisciplinary study of literary art and ethics, *Metaphor and Moral Experience* (2000).

Zina Giannopoulou is Associate Professor of Classics at the University of California, Irvine. Her research interests lie in ancient Greek philosophy (especially Plato), Greek epic and tragedy, and the reception of classical literature in the literature, film, and theater of the twentieth and twenty-first centuries. She is the author of *Plato's Theaetetus as a Second Apology* (2013).

Patrick Lee Miller is Associate Professor of Philosophy at Duquesne University, USA, where he specializes in ancient philosophy, existentialism, and psychoanalysis. His first book *Becoming God* (2011) traced the connections between reason, selfhood, and divinity in early Greek philosophy (Heraclitus through Plato). He is now working on a second volume that extends his argument into its later period (Aristotle through Plotinus). His articles on Sophocles, Nietzsche, and Freud have appeared in *Modern Psychoanalysis*, *Philosophy Today*, and *symplokē*. Online, he is a frequent contributor to *The Immanent Frame*.

Alan Nelson is Professor of Philosophy at the University of North Carolina, Chapel Hill, and Emeritus Professor of Philosophy at the University of California, Irvine. He has also taught at UCLA, USC, Stanford, and the University of Pittsburgh. His research usually focuses on early modern European philosophy. He is currently working on some problems in the development of Spinoza's thought. Since viewing *Eraserhead* in 1978, he has admired David Lynch's films so much that he finds even *Dune* to be excellent.

Robert Sinnerbrink is Senior Lecturer in Philosophy at Macquarie University, Australia. He is the author of *New Philosophies of Film: Thinking Images* (2011), *Understanding Hegelianism* (2007), co-editor of *Critique Today* (2006), and is a member of the editorial board of the journal *Film-Philosophy*. He has published numerous articles on film and philosophy, including essays on the work of David Lynch, Terrence Malick, Michael Haneke, and Lars von Trier, in journals such as *Angelaki*, *Film-Philosophy*, *Screen*, and *Screening the Past*.

F. D. Worrell researches and teaches on topics in metaethics, moral psychology, ethics, and aesthetics. He is a sometime Instructor in the Department of Philosophy and Religion at Louisiana State University and is currently a doctoral student at Tulane University, USA.

Note on the director

Born in 1946 in Missoula, Montana, David Lynch moved to Philadelphia at the age of twenty to study painting at the Pennsylvania Academy of the Fine Arts. A year later he produced his first "moving picture," the short *Six Men Getting Sick*, which was followed by *The Alphabet*, a four-minute animation financed by a grant from the American Film Institute. Having decided to pursue a career in film-making he moved to Los Angeles, where he filmed his first full-length movie, the surrealist horror *Eraserhead* (1977), which gained cult status as a midnight movie. He subsequently made *The Elephant Man* (1980), the science fiction *Dune* (1984), and the neo-noir *Blue Velvet* (1986), which was nominated for Academy Awards for best film and best director. In 1990 he made the first season of the highly popular murder mystery *Twin Peaks* for ABC (the American Broadcasting Company) (in its second season the series was cancelled by the network) and the road movie *Wild at Heart*. Two years later he released the film prequel to the television series *Twin Peaks: Fire Walk with Me*, which was poorly received by both critics and audiences. Next Lynch filmed *Lost Highway* (1996), *The Straight Story* (1999), *Mulholland Drive* (2001), for which he received the award for best director at the Cannes Film Festival and the César award for Best Foreign Film, and *Inland Empire* (2006), a nearly three-hour film in digital video.

Although he has been influenced by directors such as Stanley Kubrick, Federico Fellini, Werner Herzog, and Jacques Tati, he has created surrealist experiments of a unique style that has come to be known as "Lynchian," a mode of expression that combines the extraordinary with the ordinary, the unfamiliar with the quotidian by means of irony, dream logic, and the visual power of the unconscious.

Apart from film, Lynch has produced work in painting, drawing, photography, and sculpture, and in 2007 he published *The Air Is on Fire*, a compendium of forty years' worth of work in these media. Inspired by the artistic possibilities of the Internet, in 2002 he created a series of online shorts named *Dumbland*, as well as the surreal sitcom *Rabbits*, which he released via his website.

His many achievements include three Academy Award nominations for best director and a nomination for best screenplay, a Golden Lion award for lifetime achievement, and France's Legion of Honor.

Acknowledgments

I am grateful to C. D. C. Reeve for the invitation to contribute to the volume and the opportunity to edit it. I would like to thank Tony Bruce for his extraordinary patience and Adam Johnson for his work in producing this volume. My last thanks are reserved for all the contributors for their faith in the project and wonderful essays.

For I.Z.Δ.Γ.

If the mind is like a hall in which thought is like a voice speaking, the
voice is always that of someone else.

Wallace Stevens, "Adagia" from *Opus Posthumous*

Chapter 1

Zina Giannopoulou

INTRODUCTION

A story should have a beginning, a middle, and an end, but not necessarily in that order.

Jean-Luc Godard

DAVID LYNCH IS PERHAPS best known for his refusal to explain his films and his unorthodox film-making style. Beginning his career in fine art and mixed media, he entered mainstream movie-making at a time when it was in a state of financial and technological transformation. From his cult classic Eraserhead (1977) to his neo-noir series Twin Peaks (1990–91) to the porn video culture of Lost Highway (1997) to his abstract film Inland Empire (2006), this master of obscurantism subverts traditional approaches to narrative, plot, character development, and frame composition. Critics have responded to his films in various ways. Some regard them as works of cinematic irony that reflect upon genre, performance, and film history, requiring knowledge of narrative and genre conventions in order to be appreciated and understood. Others view his films as daring audio-visual experiments that resist rational interpretation or, dismissively, as "a shoal of red herrings, or promissory notes that cannot in the end be exchanged for anything of value."[1] Interpreters often note his engagement with the instability of identity which they study by using postmodernist (Jean Baudrillard) and psychoanalytic tools of interpretation (Jacques Lacan, Slavoj Žižek).

Others comment on his films' blend of reality and fantasy and its effect on narrative structure. For example, critics probe the indebtedness of *Mulholland Drive* to the Freudian dream-work, the ways in which the film condenses and displaces elements from reality into oneiric compositions.[2]

Mulholland Drive displays most of the cinematic tropes commonly associated with Lynch's oeuvre: non-linear patterns of exposition, intransitive narrative – in which the chain of causation that motivates the action and drives the plot is interrupted or confused through spatial and temporal fragmentation – fluid character identities, a blurry borderland between dreaming and waking life or knowledge and illusion, and loss of memory. An amnesiac car-crash victim (Laura Elena Harring) carrying only a purse with a lot of cash in it and a blue key finds her way into the apartment of an aspiring actress recently arrived in town (Naomi Watts). In what is usually thought of as the film's dream segment, the two women embark on a series of adventures evocative of the film-noir: the hunt for the amnesiac's identity, a menacing mob, marital troubles, a passionate and fragile love affair. Yet three quarters into the movie the reality segment takes over. Now the actors appear to play completely different characters, the relationships among them have changed, and nothing is as it used to be. Who are these people? What is going on? Who is dreaming whom? How much of the story is real and how much a dream? *Mulholland Drive* confronts the viewer with metaphysical, epistemological, and ethical questions to which it gives ambiguous answers.

In his introduction to the Philosophers on Film volume on *Talk to Her* Noël Carroll mentions three ways in which philosophers can engage with film: While some practice "the philosophy of the motion picture," addressing questions such as "What is the relation of film to reality?" or "What is the relation of movies to the other arts?" others explore philosophy "in" film, tackling philosophical issues which implicitly or explicitly arise on the screen. Still others show interest in "philosophy through motion pictures," seeking to show how some films, while not themselves doing philosophy, address important philosophical issues.[3] Carroll rightly suggests that these three types of film's engagement with philosophy are not mutually exclusive, and the essays in this volume bring out the force of this suggestion. The essay by Denham and Worrell, as well as that by Nelson, are poised on the threshold between "philosophy in film" and "philosophy through motion pictures."

Sinnerbrink's and Miller's essays are examples of the "philosophy in film" category, yet both view *Mulholland Drive* as an anti-philosophical work that defies rational analysis and thwarts the quest for a coherent meaning. In different ways, these philosophers explore the ways in which the film's affective power has the capacity to provoke philosophical reflection. Finally, my own essay illustrates the "philosophy of the motion picture" type while offering and defending claims that would be at home in the "philosophy in film" category. The inability of the essays in this volume to fit sharply drawn categories testifies inter alia to the complexity of *Mulholland Drive* – its narrative intricacies and visual richness. The contributors to the volume grapple with some of the film's philosophical puzzles. Although I doubt that any of these authors would claim that they have hit upon the definitive answer to the puzzles they seek to solve – indeed, the film's complex structure and the characters' identity shifts seem to compel tentative interpretations – I am confident that their essays will provoke much thought in those intrigued by the puzzles they raise. Because many of the essays include a synopsis of the film, I shall not offer one here. Instead, I shall provide an introduction to each of the essays in this collection.

In "Identity and Agency in *Mulholland Drive*," A. E. Denham and F. D. Worrell explore self-identity through the conflict between agency and necessity. Self-identity is the film's central puzzle, the insoluble mystery at the heart of the principal characters' quest. For example, although we are tempted to think that, as spatio-temporal entities, Betty and Diane are the same woman, we wonder how the naive and optimistic Betty can be the same person as the vindictive and bitter Diane. Or take Rita and Camilla. If they are one and the same person, why is Camilla a separate character, portrayed by a different actress in the film's fantasy segment? If Rita is not identical with Camilla, who was she before the car accident? Denham and Worrell argue that the protagonists of *Mulholland Drive* "do not comprise unitary, temporally continuous and internally coherent loci of agency . . . [but] are essentially fractured entities, comprising multiple and often incompatible agential structures" (p. 11). The ambiguities about their identity arise from "failures of agential unity," their inability to make reasoned choices and act on them, because of temporal, cognitive, and motivational discontinuities.

These discontinuities foreground the nature and efficacy of the characters' personal agency, an issue that Denham and Worrell pursue by posing a question that in the Western civilization originates in the works of Homer and the classical tragedians: just how much control can these fractured people exert over their fates in a universe governed by capricious chance and others' whim? How much freedom for action can there be in a world where a road accident foils a murder, the sudden appearance of a monster hiding behind a wall kills a man, and a stray bullet sets the course for the death of two innocent people? Denham and Worrell find that in such a world "the making of plans and the pursuit of goals are, at best, exercises in futility and, at worst, an unwitting conspiracy with forces which we do not understand and are helpless to control" (p. 9). Yet despite the characters' vulnerability to the vicissitudes of necessity and chance, the authors claim that Lynch's view of personal identity confirms, to a large extent, our commitment to understanding ourselves as moral agents, culpable for the choices we make; his characters "are not granted the luxury of moral innocence" (p. 12).

In his essay, "Cowboy Rules: *Mulholland Drive*, Kafka, and Illusory Freedom," Alan Nelson explores the film's treatment of human agency and freedom through a comparison with Kafka's *The Castle*. The two works are similar in many ways. In Diane's dream, Betty arrives in Los Angeles intending to pursue a career in acting, and *Mulholland Drive* is a story of the tragic frustration of her plan. There is no concrete antagonist thwarting her, instead she finds her life determined by veiled power structures whose agents appear in eerie forms. A manifestation of this power structure is her dependence on the director Adam Kesher, who is controlled by vague forces funneled through the Cowboy (who holds court at a ranch with no cows). The Cowboy appears to offer a choice – think or continue being a "smart aleck" – but the alternatives are blurry and fraught with danger. Similarly, in Kafka's story, K arrives in a new community to pursue a career as a land surveyor but is forthwith deflected from his path by mysterious forces in the inaccessible Castle. The forces are obliquely projected, as in *Mulholland Drive*, through a cast of bizarre characters. Nelson observes that Betty/Diane and K live unsettled lives as "their livelihoods, personal relationships, and even the spaces they are allowed to occupy are ephemeral" (p. 47). In Diane's dream, for example, Betty stays in her aunt's apartment, initially a place fit for a Hollywood star but eventually a refuge from sinister forces, while Adam Kesher finds his marital bed taken over by his wife's lover. Diane and Adam have problems with their love lives, and neither seems to have a financially secure job. Finally, both Diane and K are inexorably driven to their deaths. Nelson claims that under these circumstances the freedom that they enjoy is "hollow" (p. 51).

In "Mulholland Drive and Cinematic Reflexivity," I look at the relationship between film and reality from a specific angle, the connection between Lynch's film as a work of fantasy and the economic powers in charge of its materialization. This approach turns reflexivity, a film's pointing to its own fictiveness, into self-reflexivity, the ways in which Mulholland Drive comments on itself and its own production history. The feature film came out of the ashes of a television pilot that was never made because it failed to meet the producers' demands. I maintain that Lynch imports into the film the conflict between his artistic vision and executive financiers by creating in Diane an alter ego: just as he overcame fierce opposition and filmed his artistic dream so Diane dreams her version of professional and romantic success. By imaginatively refiguring key aspects of her reality Diane lives out her Hollywood dream unimpeded by external forces and populates it with surrogates who serve either as foils or as idealized versions of herself qua director and actress. By restaging its concern with the fraught relationship between economic reality and artistic fantasy her dream can be seen as a mise en abyme version of the film. Mulholland Drive thus constitutes "an ode to cinematic imagination and creativity, its ability to overcome obstacles and produce beautiful works of art" (p. 56). I also defend a quadripartite structure of the film that stresses the temporal dimension of Diane's life and calls attention to another reflexive element of the movie, the subjection of its main protagonist to the gaze, whether her own or Lynch's.

In writing his essay, "Silencio: Mulholland Drive as Cinematic Romanticism," Robert Sinnerbrink draws inspiration from the early German romantics, specifically their notion of "transcendental irony," the attainment by literary works of a unity of thought and imagination through the overcoming of the divisions between philosophy and literature, universal and particular, reason and feeling. He foregrounds the immensely affective power of Lynch's films and sees Mulholland Drive as a neo-romantic work that is expressive and reflective at once by combining aesthetic sensation and philosophical reflection. In his view, the movie is characterized "by its striking conjunction of sensuous intensity and reflective complexity," while its deepest mystery lies "in its capacity to express and elicit mood, affect, and aesthetic reflection in a fragmentary work that both invites and resists philosophical interpretation" (p. 79). He argues that the film thwarts cognitive or conceptual closure through the elicitation of an "enveloping or *autonomous mood* sequence," namely a stylized mood sequence that all but eclipses narrative content in favor of sensation and affect, while at the same time opening up thought and reflection through cinematic means (p. 84). The best example of this kind of sequence is Club Silencio, which Sinnerbrink sees as an example of cinematic romanticism, an autonomous mood sequence that integrates "affective, intuitive, and reflective expression," taps into the conscious and unconscious mind, and comments on the history of Hollywood movies (p. 77). *Mulholland Drive* thus seems to exist in what Stanley Cavell calls "the condition of modernism" or "film in the condition of philosophy," a film reflecting on its own historical and material conditions as a work of art.

Patrick Lee Miller, in his essay, "Monstrous Maturity on Mulholland Dr.," observes that Lynch exhorts his viewers to "feel" his films and to refrain from trying to understand them. Miller stages a rivalry between two ways of understanding tragic drama – Plato's and Nietzsche's – and interprets *Mulholland Drive* as a fulfillment of the second. On this account, Plato diminishes imagination in general, rejects tragedy in particular, and enjoins us to subdue the irrational emotions elicited by both; his goal is to understand a reality that is pure being, free of contradiction, and eternally consistent. By contrast, Nietzsche teaches us to feel, and thereby understand, the horror of impure becoming through the beautiful appearance of tragic art. In order to understand this public dream of a film and ourselves as its communal dreamers, Miller enjoins us to disregard Plato's concern for consistency and instead, like Nietzsche, distinguish between those dreams that are beautiful, creative, and vital, and those that are ugly, destructive, and morbid. By subverting the distinction between appearance and reality, by dissolving the identities of the characters who move in its twilight, and by putting a monster at the terminus of their search for pure reality, this film dramatizes something like the elements of Nietzsche – his tragic epistemology and the anti-Platonic trajectory of his education. Miller argues that Lynch manages not only to enact these elements but also to present them as a distinctive lesson about our own selves: we are each a dramaturge, he claims, and we mature not when we cancel the show to escape the cinema into the noonday sun, but when we focus the camera long enough to improvise something that sublimates our longings for beauty and love. Maturity is not waking from our dreams, but dreaming ones that are beautiful.

Notes

1   Nicholas Lezard, "David Lynch: Director of Dreams," *Guardian*, 17 February 2012, <http://www.guardian.co.uk/film/2012/feb/17/david-lynch-film-director-dreams>.
2   See, among others, Roger F. Cook, "Hollywood Narrative and the Play of Fantasy: David Lynch's *Mulholland Drive*," *Quarterly Review of Film and Video* 28 (2011): 369–81.
3   Noël Carroll, "Talk to Them: An Introduction," in A. W. Eaton (ed.), *Talk to Her* (London: Routledge, 2008), pp. 1–10.

Chapter 2

A. E. Denham and F. D. Worrell

IDENTITY AND AGENCY IN *MULHOLLAND DRIVE*

> . . . [W]hat is great is fragile, and what is necessary may be destructive.
>
> (Williams 1993: 253)

MULHOLLAND DRIVE CONFRONTS the viewer with persistent questions concerning identity. Its protagonists – the dual personae of Betty/Diane and Rita/Camilla – appear in different roles at different times and places, participating in different stories, and the identities of the characters with whom they interact are often similarly ambiguous. Just who are these people and how are they related each to the other? Are Betty and Diane numerically identical – one and the same woman – or different women with overlapping histories? If the former, why are they so radically different in their actions and attitudes? If the latter, why does the same actress play both parts? What of Rita and Camilla? If Rita and Camilla are one and the same, why is Camilla an entirely separate character portrayed by a different actress in the narrative's first story? If not, again, why have the same actress play both parts in other episodes? And if Rita isn't identical with Camilla, who was Rita before she is stricken with amnesia?

The narrative thread of *Mulholland Drive* is woven of such questions. Indeed, the plot of the first narrative develops the mystery of Rita's identity, and the dangers associated with its discovery, as well as the subnarrative investigating the identity of the elusive Diane Selwyn. Lynch compels us to travel with his characters through their confusion and uncertainty, presenting a narrative in which we, too, are made to wonder who they are — to ask how they are related one to another, when and where they are located, and, above all, whether they are real or imagined, or both.

Alongside the ambiguities surrounding his characters' identities, Lynch's narrative provokes questions about the control, or want of control, they exercise over their fates — questions concerning the nature and efficacy of their personal agency. It seems to be a tale (or two) of plans gone wrong: its principal characters find their projects subverted, their intentions frustrated, and their choices undermined. Obstacles to the will confront them at every turn, raised alternately by the tyranny of others' schemes or the caprice of chance: freakish accidents foil well-designed murders, despised encounters lead to love, stray bullets and bad dreams set the course for sudden death. Almost nothing turns out as its characters expect, and the overall trajectory of events suggests that the making of plans and the pursuit of goals are, at best, exercises in futility and, at worst, an unwitting conspiracy with forces which we do not understand and are helpless to control.

In this respect *Mulholland Drive* continues a long tradition of literary tales charting the conflict between agency and necessity — a tradition dating back to Homer and the classical tragedians, whose protagonists' attempts at mastering their fates are repeatedly frustrated in ways that challenge what they can do and who they really are. The precise dynamics of tragic conflict are subtle and complicated. The best tragedies do not deliver simple accounts of "internal will" versus "external compulsion." Rather, they show how difficult it often is to unravel a clear account of either causal or moral responsibility. Just behind the external necessities imposed on the tragic protagonist — however powerful and onerous they may be — lurks the causal force of his own, individual character: motivations and desires which he may not endorse, and may not even consciously acknowledge, nonetheless drive his choices. In the tragedies of Aeschylus, Sophocles, and Euripides there is always an intelligible sense in which the tragic protagonist could have *acted* otherwise, had he *been* otherwise — say, had he been a person of different character or temperament or destiny. Consider Ajax: his competitiveness and love of honor led him to plot the slaughter of his commanders in revenge for being denied Achilles' armor; it was to prevent the realization of this (genuine) choice that Athena deprives him of his reason and bestows the madness that is his ruin. Or consider Pentheus, an impetuous, unreflective youth ruled by transitory desires. Unable to regulate his curiosity (perhaps especially his sexual curiosity), he is tempted by Dionysus' lures, and thus falls victim to the Bacchantes' murderous rage.

This ambiguous interplay between external and internal necessity is a mark of all classical tragedies. Different as they are, they share a common, disturbing moral dynamic: the agent's wrongdoings and their disastrous consequences are, on the one hand, unavoidable; on the other hand, their causal lineage is too readily traceable to the agent's own character and choices to be entirely disowned. Such relations of identity, agency, and necessity are what finally set a tragic drama apart from a mere tale of misfortune: the tragic drama turns on the tension between our conception of ourselves as determining (and answerable for) the course of our lives, on the one hand, and as determined by (and hence helpless before) necessities which we are powerless to change. All of the various particular narratives of classical tragedy, in one way or another, unfold this universal conflict. As Jean-Pierre Vernant comments,

> In the tragic perspective, acting, being an agent, has a double character. On the one side, it consists in taking council with oneself, weighing the for and against and doing the best one can to foresee the order of means and ends. On the other hand, it is to make a bet on the unknown and the incomprehensible and to take a risk on a terrain that remains impenetrable to you.
>
> (Vernant and Vidal-Naquet 1981: 37)

The protagonists of a tragic drama are always thus suspended between personal agency and inscrutable forces that lie beyond their understanding and control. The narrative unfolding of events is at once an unfolding of forces independent of the agent and the agent's own internal psychology – of who he inevitably is, and what he must inevitably do. Thus causal laws, destiny, and sheer luck are interwoven with personal choice into a fabric that is unpredictable and ultimately unmanageable. The forces of fate are fearful, and we are to be pitied for our vulnerability to them; but perhaps even more fearful and pitiable is the unwitting compliance of our own natures in destroying our best efforts to master our lives.

A quintessentially contemporary film in some respects, Mulholland Drive exploits the dynamics of ancient tragedies to similarly challenge the optimistic thought that the history of human agency is one of continuously improved autonomy and control. Do we now really understand our own psychologies, our capacity for agency, and the conditions of autonomy better than our ancient ancestors? Have we, by better articulating our image of ourselves as rational actors, and by rejecting supernatural metaphysics, really defeated the irrational forces that once shaped our lives and determined our happiness? Or are we, much like Agamemnon, Antigone, and Pentheus, still suspended precariously between faith in our moral autonomy, and skepticism that it can survive the pressures that surround it?

Locating Mulholland Drive in the tragic tradition, we trace its account of and responses to these long-standing questions. More specifically, we argue that the puzzles the film poses about identity arise directly from Lynch's view of the boundaries, nature, and, finally, the reality of human agency. We proceed in three parts. The first turns to these central concepts directly, sketching a theoretical framework for their contents and relations within which the perspective of practical reason – the standpoint from which we judge what to do and why – requires that we conceive of ourselves as unified agents. The second part turns to the details of the film, and in particular its images of what we call "agential fragmentation." A person's agency is fragmented in so far as its normal unity is disrupted by discontinuities and incoherencies internal to his own psychological constitution. As Lynch profiles Mulholland Drive's protagonists, we argue, they do not comprise unitary, temporally continuous and internally coherent loci of agency. Rather, they are essentially fractured entities, comprising multiple and often incompatible agential structures. The ambiguities about their identity arise from within their psychological constitutions – in particular, from failures of agential unity. Such failures, moreover, constitute one kind of tragic necessity in the sense that they are unbidden, involuntary, and authoritative.

The third turns to a different form of necessity: "agential nullification." Here, the sources of interference with agential unity – principally chance and externally determined fate – do not so much disrupt the agent's ability to make genuine choices as enact them. In agential nullification, certain outcomes are imposed upon a character irrespective of what he does. True to Vernant's "double character" of tragic agency, the principal characters of *Mulholland Drive* repeatedly find their agency undermined in this way: external powers manipulate, coerce, and destroy them, just as the gods destroy the tragic Greek protagonists.[1] Yet Lynch allows suspicions to linger about the characters' accountability for the outcomes in which they play a role; they are not granted the luxury of moral innocence. They do not plan, and do not intend, those outcomes; yet they are instrumental in bringing them about, unwittingly conspiring with daemonic fate.

Identity and agential unity

If *Mulholland Drive* is a tragedy, it should be unsurprising that it poses problems of identity, for these are inextricably bound up with the nature and scope of human agency. Before turning to the details of the film, let us first reflect briefly on how these two properties – identity and agency – interact.

When we ask whether someone may be held accountable for a certain event or outcome, we typically assume that his actions at least played a causal role in bringing them about; but we also typically make two further assumptions. One is that the person is capable of genuine action – that he is, for instance, a person whose behaviors can be explained in terms of beliefs, desires, reasons, and intentions, rather than as mere effects of antecedent causes. (When Ajax is rendered delusional by Athena and proceeds to slaughter the Achaeans' livestock, is this action truly his – is it the action of a *person* at all, or mere behavior, to be causally explained in other terms?) The other assumption we must make is that the person to whom we *now* refer as the agent is, at the least, one and the same as the agent of the past actions in question. (Again: is Ajax, at the point of his act of slaughter, then properly "himself" – identical with the non-delusional Ajax who had plotted instead to murder Odysseus? If not, who is he?) In short, the conditions of identity figure among the indispensable conditions of accountable agency. (If it was not so-and-so who then acted, how can so-and-so be the agent of what ensued?) This is one obvious and familiar way in which identity and agency are intertwined.

We may also wonder whether agency is not itself a condition of identity. Tragic protagonists are sometimes transformed not by divine forces but by internal ones: Creon confesses that he was possessed by pride and anger (his own, presumably) when he ordered the death of his dear niece. Agamemnon, too, laments that in his role as a commander he must cease thinking and choosing as Iphigenia's father; another set of motivations is proper to that role, and his daughter is sacrificed. To be sure, whether the forces undermining agency are external and distant (the will of Athena or Dionysus) or internal and proximate (Creon's royal pride and Agamemnon's passion for victory), they work by challenging the agent's psychological continuity: they change what he does and who he is in ways that disrupt the connectedness and coherence of his beliefs, desires, and intentions and so undermine the unity of his practical reasoning. But where the sources of discontinuity are internal to the agent's own psychology is it not the fragmentation of personal agency which challenges our judgements of personal identity, and not the other way around? Questions of personal identity sometimes arise just *because* of discontinuities in our exercises of agency – fractures in our patterns of practical reasoning and the actions they recommend. Unities and disunities of agency, in short, guide our practices of identifying and individuating persons.

Let us try to capture this point more precisely by considering what is built into the notions of "identity" and "agency." Questions of identity can be addressed in both diachronic and synchronic terms. Synchronic identity asks what makes us the person we are at any given time as opposed to any other person. How might we differentiate ourselves from others? What characteristics make me the unique individual that I am?[2] While there is no consensus among philosophers about the details of a correct account of synchronic identity, certain properties are likely necessary ones: a single stream of consciousness, uniqueness of experiential memory, unique personality and projects, etc.[3] Here, we take such general conditions to be indispensable, and nothing will turn on commitments to a more specific or complete account of synchronic identity.

The problem of diachronic identity, while closely related, is importantly different: it concerns the changes through which someone may persist while remaining the same person. In general, and on the view at work here, diachronic identity depends in various ways on degrees of psychological continuity.[4] That is, the person you are at an earlier time counts as identical to – is the same person as – the person you are at a later time just if they are sufficiently psychologically continuous. No doubt, there are some cases in which it is simply indeterminate whether two temporally independent identifications are identifications of the "same person."[5] Nonetheless, in many − indeed most − cases psychological continuities underpin our everyday judgements of diachronic identity. What, however, counts as "sufficiently psychologically continuous"?

Psychological continuity occurs along different psychological characteristics, which may be individuated in different ways. Several kinds of continuity are clearly relevant, falling into two broad categories − what we may call "cognitive" and "motivational" continuities. In the cognitive category, one important dimension is continuity of memory, perhaps especially experiential or episodic memory, such that past experiences are remembered first-personally by your present self. Further, there are continuities of assertoric beliefs − that $2 + 2 = 4$, or that England has a rainy climate − and of knowledge-based abilities or "knowledge-how," such as knowing how to play the piano or to drive a motor car.

These cognitive continuities are all pertinent to judgements of diachronic identity, but they are not, on their own, wholly decisive. Sometimes of equal importance are the motivational continuities: one's desires, hopes, fears, loves, and aversions and one's temperament or affective disposition, such as being affectionate or having a ready sense of humor. These continuities are closely related to a further one − continuity of intention and enactment, such that when you intend to do something at one time, you subsequently enact that intention. Now, suppose that your memories remain intact, and your avowed beliefs remain stable, but you begin to manifest a very different temperament, emotional dispositions, and personal tastes. Do you remain the same person if you are radically altered in this way? What if, additionally, your wider outlook and attitude toward life changed radically, so that you no longer endorsed the same evaluative norms, personal goals, and guiding principles? Are you the same individual after such changes as you were before? Such changes would normally be accompanied by discontinuities in intention and action as well: your prior intentions are never fulfilled, and new intentions are formed which would never have been supported by your earlier desires and evaluations. The person you are now enacts a very different pattern of choices than the person you previously were.

We suggested earlier that notions of agency and identity are closely interwoven, and that disruption or fragmentation of the former can give us reason to doubt our judgements of the latter. Now we can say why this is so: it is because problems of diachronic identity closely track agential capacities – a person's ability to originate reasoned choices and to impose those choices on the world. Like diachronic identity, personal agency depends on continuities or unity in two temporal directions: backward, into the agent's past (his memories, his established beliefs, his acquired abilities) and forward, into his future (his intentions, plans, aims, and goals). And again like diachronic identity, personal agency depends essentially on both cognitive and motivational continuities. Consider a simple case in which you originate and realize a choice, say, between travelling by the low road or the high road. In order to choose between these alternatives, you need to remember both routes, have access to beliefs about their characteristics, be able to rely on your driving abilities to negotiate these roads, be motivated to prefer one to the other and, finally, you must be capable of forming and acting upon an intention to take one route or the other. Deficits in any of these conditions of continuity will interfere with your agential control of the circumstances, leaving you either incapable of making a choice or incapable of realizing it. The internal, causal conditions of personal agency – the psychological capacities you require to perform an *action* (rather than, as is sometimes said, a "mere act") – include *temporal unity* across all of these dimensions. The conditions of agency in this respect overlap with the conditions of diachronic personal identity, as well as the other way around: they stand or fall together.

Considerations such as these have led some to suggest that it is the unity of agency that grounds or gives rise to the very idea of diachronic personal identity – of a person as a unified subject of experience, persisting through time. The thought is that this idea would gain no purchase at all but for the fact that we conceive of ourselves and live our lives from the practical standpoint of self-directing, deliberative agents. As Korsgaard puts the point,

> Communication and functional integration do not require a common subject of conscious experiences. What they do require, however, is the unity of agency ... when I engage in psychic activities deliberately, I regard myself as the subject of these activities. I think,

I look, I try to remember. But this is just the second element of the
unity of agency, the unity inherent in the deliberative standpoint.

(Korsgaard 1989: 377)

Put simply, Korsgaard's claim is that we regard ourselves as unified
subjects – as having individual, personal identities at all – only because
we conceive of ourselves as agents who must deliberate, choose, and
enact our choices. It is this *practical* requirement of agency that generates
and grounds the idea that there is "someone within" who acts: a unique,
persisting, and unchanging self. In so far as we are tempted to conceive
of ourselves in this way, we do so because it falls to us to live as agents,
destined by our natures to think of ourselves as unified, originating
sources of choices, actions, and conditions of the world.[6]

Agential fragmentation

Is the very idea of a temporally persisting, unique, individual person
mistaken? Do we mistakenly infer from the practical necessity of our unity
as agents to the metaphysical necessity of a special kind of entity – a
unified, Cartesian self? Might there be no one and nothing constituting
who or what each of us is? Is there perhaps nothing *more* to being a
unique, individual person beyond the psychological continuities requisite
for our everyday attempts to chart a course for ourselves in the world?[7]

Our aim here is neither to defend nor to deny any particular
metaphysical conception of identity or agency. But we do aim to better
understand how these notions are articulated and related in *Mulholland Drive*,
and to do so in ways consistent with its formal affinities with the
tradition of tragic drama. To that end, the psychological conception of
identity just sketched delivers a framework within which the film's
different – and otherwise quite disparate – narrative parts pull together
in an identifiable theoretical direction. We are not suggesting, of course,
that Lynch aimed to illustrate any particular metaphysical thesis, let alone
to *argue* for one. *Mulholland Drive* is a work of cinematic art, and a good
one: it is neither didactic nor transparent. But, like the best philosophical
arguments, it elicits responses, which are not only metaphysically
unsettling but also theoretically coherent.

One way in which Lynch provokes questions about the identity of his
characters is by disrupting the continuity and order of the spatial and

temporal contexts in which they are presented. In parallel with these dislocations, however, it presents characters who themselves lack unity: their cognitive capacities and their motivational sets are deprived of various essential continuities, fracturing their agential identities. They are also agentially incoherent, in the sense that their different agential profiles – the different fragments, as it were, of their agential profiles – prescribe different and incompatible values, goals, and projects. Lynch achieves this by various devices. First and most obviously, the film's two narratives feature two central protagonists bearing different names: Rita/Camilla and Betty/Diane. These composite characters represent two versions of what we refer to as "agential fragmentation," or fractured agency. We discuss each in turn.

Rita/Camilla is first introduced in the role of a passive victim: a lone woman riding in a car on a dark and dangerous road, driven by two anonymous men deputed to murder her. She is saved by a freakish accident, which she survives. But her survival is importantly incomplete: the person who walks away from the burning wreckage is an amnesiac, deprived of her entire past and hence of her ability to shape her future in the normal ways. Her initial actions are guided, not as a *person's* would be – with intent and by way of a goal or aim or plan – but by animal instinct: she is drawn unthinkingly towards distant lights and moves numbly towards them through the wilderness of the surrounding hills, she hides in a nest of foliage, she succumbs to sleep. When daylight breaks, she seeks out a place to hide, where she sleeps again. On her discovery by Betty, Rita arbitrarily chooses a name from a film poster of Rita Hayworth and pretends to a fictive identity.[8] However, she soon tearfully confesses her plight: "I don't know who I am."

Lynch's choice of Rita's role of amnesiac is well judged, if his intent is to present a character whose agential capacities fail to be properly integrated. It is well known that amnesiacs who suffer radical losses of both experiential and indirect memories suffer other deficits as well – specifically, deficits in agential abilities to form intentions, to identify goals, make plans, or deliberate about the future. In sum, they have great difficulties in making choices or decisions and generating practical judgements. This does not seem to be owed to any deficits in general capacities for reasoning: studies of amnesiacs reveal no deficits in their performance on categorization tasks or their ability to apply rules to particular cases, despite having no recollection of previous applications, nor, in some cases, any ability to retain the rule for future ones. Rather, it is as if in losing their past they also lose some of their grasp of the future. This is borne out by a study showing that they perform poorly on the Iowa Gambling Task.[9] Moreover, when performing that task amnesiacs – like many patients with ventromedial damage – fail to show anticipatory skin-conductance responses to either advantageous or disadvantageous decks. (Indeed, classic amnesiac cases typically result from medial or frontal lobe damage, which is known to impair executive functioning.) Philip Gerrans and Jeanette Kennett speculate that amnesiacs suffer, not only from an inability to retrieve their experiential past, but from a more global dysfunction of their capacity for "mental time travel" – "the ability to retrieve past episodes and imagine future ones and to integrate the results with other forms of knowledge as part of planning" (Gerrans and Kennett 2010: 598). Certainly in Rita's character we find someone who is impaired both in her access to previous times and in her ability to actively choose the shape of future ones: she repeatedly hesitates when Betty proposes plans or schemes to aid her, she follows directions in a quite passive, childlike manner, and she proposes no agendas of her own. She seems able to act only when driven by an immediate desire or impulse – to sleep, to wash, to eat, to make love. These are actions, to be sure, but they do not add up to agency in the full sense that is required to lead a connected, unified life out of which one might construct a continuous autobiography. Autobiographies occur across time, and by way of connections forged between past, present, and future. In this respect they are creations of mental time travel, as we move backwards and forwards in thought, intention, and action. A mere capacity to respond to transitory impulses and desires will not do the trick: for an act to count as expressing personal agency, those responses need to be sensitive to reasons supplied by past experience and anticipations of the future: in short, they need to express intentions informed by the requisite *cognitive continuities*. As Gerrans and Kennett comment:

> Planning requires a capacity to imaginatively project oneself into the future; this in turn requires both a sense of oneself as the very same individual who will inhabit that future . . . and also the kind of detailed self-knowledge that is supported by autobiographical memory. We exercise the capacity for mental time travel whenever

we revise for this year a class we gave last year – remembering what worked and what didn't – whenever we reflect on what kind of career or job would best suit us, whenever we plan a holiday or a shopping trip, arrange a meeting, organize a party, or commit ourselves to a course of study, an exercise program, or a marriage. In so committing ourselves . . . we provide reasons for ourselves in the future, reasons which will be ours, but which we would otherwise not have had. In this way we construct ourselves as particular, temporally extended, agents. Our diachronic reasons, made salient to us via our capacity for mental time travel, are thus in a position to compete with synchronically occurring wants.

(Gerrans and Kennett 2010: 601–2)

Lynch's Rita is not a person who organizes, arranges, plans, or commits. Thus, as Gerrans and Kennett's comment implies, she in one sense is not a person at all; she is so incapable of normal patterns of reflection and deliberation that she fails to act on reasons – she fails to qualify as a properly rational being.

Is this character a construction of the later Diane's wishful fantasies? When we turn to the second narrative and encounter the very different, agentially robust Camilla, it is not difficult to appreciate why this might be so. Camilla is presented as the counterpart of Rita in the second narrative: both characters are played by Laura Elena Harring, each is romantically involved with one of the Betty/Diane characters, and both characters have attempts made on their lives. In the second narrative, Camilla is presented as a bisexual vixen, prepared to marry a man while pursuing women, and to use her faux commitment to her husband as a smokescreen for her infidelity and indifference to Diane. (It is easy enough to read her bisexuality as itself a set of contradictory impulses.) Alternatively, if we suppose that Camilla really does abandon Diane because of her relationship with Adam, this yields another signal of moral viciousness, for on the night they are to (presumably) announce their engagement we see her seductively kissing another woman. Somewhere torn between genders and commitments, hedonistic passions and cold indifference sits Camilla – an utterly different woman, motivated by utterly different passions, virtues, and vices, from the Rita of Diane's dreams.[10] Camilla is everything that Rita is not in these respects: she is presented as not merely planning but scheming, as not only arranging but manipulating, and she does not so much organize her life as orchestrate it – with others as her instruments. The characters who fall within her orbit are all used as means to her ends: Adam and Diane most obviously, but even the female lover whom she kisses at the dinner is, it seems, being used as a vehicle to provoke jealousy.[11] No one escapes Camilla's web of calculations. Indeed, in the end she becomes almost as much the agent of *Diane's* life as of her own, and is finally implicated in Diane's death as well. Where Rita is a fractured agent, whose capacity for genuine action is disrupted and discontinuous, lacking the requisite cognitive connectedness to plan and lead any kind of normal life, Camilla is an über-agent – subject to no one's will and free to direct the affections and actions of others to her own ends. Or so she is until she meets her fate at gunpoint – a fate which her own internal necessities were complicit in creating.

Mulholland Drive offers a parallel dynamic of fractured agency yielding disintegrated identity in the character of Betty/Diane. There are strong indications that Betty and Diane are, in spatial and temporal terms, the same embodied woman: as mere spatio-temporal occupants, they are numerically identical. Naomi Watts plays both characters; Betty vanishes before Diane appears; the two have the same personal histories. On other levels too, the viewer is invited to identify them: they share the same wider ambitions. Betty/Diane seems to be two profiles of a single woman – an aspiring young actress presented by way of two personae, within two, contemporaneous biographical episodes. In both profiles, Betty/Diane is in love with another woman – the further double persona of Rita/Camilla. Countless minor biographical overlaps work to establish the common identity of Betty/Diane as a temporally and spatially continuous individual. There seems to be little question, in short, that they represent different possible realizations of the life of a single physical being.

Yet, in other ways the viewer is invited to wonder at how they could be the same person. How could Betty ever become Diane? The first and second incarnations of each possess utterly different characters. The first biography, commonly interpreted as the actress's idealized, fantasy self, tells a tale in which a well-meaning, naive, and optimistic young woman assists an amnesiac in her search for her identity. In this tale, Betty is a young woman of high principles, grand ambitions, and tender feelings, naturally given to thinking the best of other people.[12] The second biography tells a much darker tale. Here, Betty/Diane suffers rejection by Rita/Camilla – the latter now a cold-hearted, manipulative tease who calculatingly arranges scenarios to humiliate and enrage her lovers. Diane, in her unraveled and desperate state, has Camilla murdered and then kills herself, wracked by grief and terror.

Between the two narratives, in which Betty reappears as Diane, she is utterly transformed. Betty's innocence gives way to Diane's bitterness, her benevolence to malice, her tenderness to jealously, her energy and enthusiasm to lethargy and despair, her hopefulness to cynicism, and, finally, her reasonableness and inner calm to terrified delusions. Betty's moral character is very far removed from that of her incarnation as Diane; one might say that the key difference between them is that the latter has lost her moral compass altogether. There are other differences too, essential to identity: emotional differences in Betty's and Diane's receptivity to love, their sociability, and their susceptibility to self-deceit. It is no accident, perhaps, that Diane's disaffected persona sees the ugly truth of her circumstances all too clearly, while Betty, her happier alter ego, is given to consoling illusions. After all, motivational and cognitive states are notoriously interdependent: our desires all too often drive our beliefs.

Which of the protagonists, the film prompts one to ask, is the real person and which the illusion? The first, to be sure, may be a dream. Lynch's narrative includes several instances of characters drifting into sleep or awaking from sleep, and an early scene in which Dan relates his preoccupation with a recurring nightmare places this theme at the fore.[13] The evidence that Betty is an imagined persona – the "unreal" person – is substantial. The film opens with a point-of-view shot that ends buried in a pillow on Diane Selwyn's bed, and the first narrative closes with Diane being "awakened" by the Cowboy, an almost supernatural figure. Hence, the entire first narrative might be a dream of Diane's making, manifesting as dreams do both her wishes and her fears.[14]

It is also telling that Naomi Watts hideously overacts while playing Betty – clearly a directorial choice on Lynch's part, since her performance is nuanced and subtle elsewhere in the film. Every one of Betty's lines is delivered with excessive zeal and emotion, except during one scene; much of the time, her character is almost Brechtian in its thinness and one-dimensional form.[15] Moreover, Betty is – interestingly, in this context – a passive recipient in many respects: she just happens upon Rita, her aunt arranges her audition, she follows the male actor's lead in how she plays her audition scene (and does so very differently than when rehearsing with Rita). Even the role for which she auditions is that of a vulnerable young woman of whom an older man takes advantage. In her relations with Rita, where she manifests greater agency, she is still very often more led than leading; it is Rita's difficulties which set the dominant agenda, Rita who initiates their love-making, and Rita who takes her to the Club Silencio. In fact, Betty's personal goals are consistently neglected for Rita's sake: she leaves the set of The Sylvia North Story before being introduced to Adam in order to track Diane Selwyn with Rita, she ignores the wishes of her aunt and lets Rita stay in the apartment, and ignores the obvious warning signs that all is not what it seems with Rita – the money and the secrecy of the police. Betty is most capable of exercising agency and will, in fact, when she is making choices on Rita's behalf. Then, she insists on ringing the police, on tracking down Diane Selwyn, on climbing through the window into Diane's apartment. It is as if in Betty's dream, she is the agent of nothing – perhaps is nothing – save as a vehicle of Rita's needs.

All told, there is something very contrived about Betty's character, as bad fiction is contrived. The viewer knows, and is meant to know, that Watts is play-acting when we watch Betty. We are meant to be aware that everything Betty says is scripted, preordained by an idealized paradigm that lacks the texture, substance, and complexity of real life. Betty is surely not a real person – she is a caricature, a fantasy of Diane's memories of her youthful self. Betty is an exaggeration, a hyperbole of the imagination.

Diane is not, given the account of identity sketched earlier, the same person as Betty. Betty is so radically divergent in attitude, outlook, and agenda that she could not possibly be Diane. But matters are not, in fact, so simple: in another sense, Betty is Diane – as Diane recalls her former self. Diane is imagining who she once was – young, healthy, naive, and uncorrupted by temptations and disappointment. (Perhaps, one reason that Rita is an amnesiac in this dream/fantasy is because the young Diane at the time did not know how Camilla would eventually affect her.) Yet Betty is not completely lost to Diane; we see flashes of Betty's hopefulness shine through Diane's depression and cynicism: Diane initially glows at encountering an hallucination of Camilla; she is also disarmed when

Camilla surprises her by appearing from the woods to lead her to Adam's home on Mulholland Dr. Perhaps most significantly, Diane is finally driven to suicide, perhaps not only by fear but also by confusion, guilt, and remorse. Surely the cold-blooded, murderous Diane is not the source of such emotions? The moral emotions can only be had by a person with a moral compass, a person who has not yet lost her soul to Hollywood and the world. These belong to Betty, not Diane.

So Betty survives in certain respects in Diane. Moreover, even if Betty is only a dream of Diane's making, it is a dream drawing in part on first-personal memories of Diane as once she was (or imagined herself to be) – before she was deformed by the base machinations of Hollywood and the complex emotions of a failed love affair. This much is clear from the events and characters which overlap both narratives, and to the extent that it draws on biographical fact, it is more than mere fantasy. One must bear in mind, too, that dreams reveal much about the dreamer: in particular, one learns of one's wishes and fears from them. If the first narrative is a dream, then it tells us as much about Diane as it does about Betty, her fantasy self. It is hard to resist seeing the generous, hopeful, and talented Betty as the woman Diane still longs to be, and Betty's life as the one she longs to lead – a life with a promising future in both work and love, and in which she is Camilla's lover and benefactor, rather than her murderer.

Any answer to the questions "Which is the real person?" and "Are these two the same person?" will depend in part on how each character is identified in the first place. If we are defined by our memories, our hopes, and our evaluative ideals, then Betty is a possible manifestation of the "real" Diane. Betty and Diane are the same person in respect of many physical and some cognitive continuities, but distinct with respect to others – to moral values, to the dominance of various emotions, to intentions in love. The features with respect to which they differ are principally – although not solely – features of their motivational sets: their aims and intentions, evaluations, dominating passions, desires, wishes, and fears. Diane, like Rita and many characters in Lynch's other works, is a house divided, a duality of radically divergent passions and values. This dual-protagonist is at once a ball of sorrow and a ball of hope, a murderess and a suicide, a benevolent Samaritan and a vengeful amoralist.[16]

Whether or not Rita/Camilla and Betty/Diane are judged to be the same person, they are clearly very different *agents*, responsive to different reasons, driven by different desires, making their choices and guiding their lives by different purposes and ideals. By offering them different names and locating them in different narratives, Lynch invites us to wonder whether anything like a continuous, unified person can survive such fracturing of agency. We earlier sketched a philosophical thesis according to which it is the practical requirement of unity in agency – the need, in practice, to conceive of ourselves as unified in order to live as agents at all – which accounts for our metaphysical notion of a persisting and unified subject, a unique and particular self. In Lynch's two protagonists, we encounter fragmented agents: selves which have lost, in different ways and for different reasons, that requisite practical agential unity. Unbidden, uncontrolled features of their own psychologies – both cognitive and motivational – usurp authority over their practical judgements, and undermine their ability to steer their lives along a coherent and integrated course. Do they, then, survive as persons at all?

Agential nullification

> Man, when running over, frequently without his own knowledge, frequently in spite of himself, the route which nature has marked out for him, resembles a swimmer who is obliged to follow the current that carries him along; he believes himself a free agent because he sometimes consents, sometimes does not consent, to glide with the stream, which, notwithstanding, always hurries him forward.
>
> (Holbach 1770: 177)

Mulholland Drive shows us that when our psychological unity is subverted we are, or can become, fragmentary agents: we change over time in alarmingly disparate ways, while pressing forward towards our ends as if we were traversing a single, unified trajectory. This is one way in which the film articulates the conflict between agency and necessity, and the implications of that conflict for our understanding of just who and what we are.

The evidence of common experience indicates that our practical agency is often disrupted in other ways as well, however. Even when our practical judgements issue from a relatively continuous and coherent internal psychology, they are often frustrated at the point of enactment by external obstacles that are unbidden, unwelcome, and beyond our rational control. Lynch is sensitive to these other sources of necessity, and the subplots of Mulholland Drive reflect them, focusing (like traditional tragedies) on those of chance or luck, on the one hand, and destiny, on the other. These are the modern-day "puppeteers" of everyday life, nullifying even our best-laid plans and most rational choices, and they are cast by Lynch in roles of almost supernatural authority.

The authority of chance is introduced early on in the first narrative, when Rita's imminent death (a carefully designed murder) is interrupted by a bizarre crash. (Some daredevil teenagers speeding along Mulholland Dr. collide with Rita's assassins' car, sending all save Rita to their deaths.) The viewer is thus put on his guard at the outset: anything can happen at any time, and what seems inevitable at one moment can become impossible the next.

This idea is later elaborated in the comical scene in which Joe, himself a hired killer, murders Ed, his sometime friend, in order to secure a "black book" of valuable (presumably criminal) information. The scene opens with Joe and Ed in friendly conversation, glibly mocking a "totally freak accident" – presumably the very accident which in the first narrative spares Rita's life. After successfully shooting Ed, Joe attempts to stage the scene as a suicide. To leave powder burns on Ed's hand, Joe fires a second shot into the wall. This shot, however, hits a woman working in the next-door office, whom Ed must then also kill – but not until after a janitor has witnessed him assaulting her. All told, he shoots two people who were never his intended targets, and these shots in turn start a fire and set off the building alarm system, compelling Joe to flee in a panic. The originating author of these absurd events is mere chance or random bad luck: two innocents die, simply because they are in the wrong place at the wrong time. (Had the woman's chair been moved forward only a few inches, her life would have been spared; had the janitor gone to vacuum a different floor, he might have survived as well.)[17]

One cannot but be reminded, in this context, of Oedipus' chance encounter with Laius on the road to Thebes. Suppose that Laius had not set out on that particular day, or met Oedipus on that particular stretch of the road, and spoken to him in quite that contemptuous tone? Mere chance dovetails with our natures to transform us into the agents of events we do not intend, cannot endorse, and can never control. We plan, we orchestrate, we design. But what these exercises of agency ultimately yield is something that we both do and do not do, making us into what we are – and are not. At the same time, Oedipus, like Ed, is not blameless. He did what he did, and his role in the killing calls a pollution upon Thebes. As Bernard Williams commented:

> . . . [I]t is something that has happened to him, but at the same time it may be something that he brought about. *What has happened to him, in fact, is that he has brought it about* . . . The terrible thing that happened to him, through no fault of his own, was that he did these things.
>
> (Williams 1993: 70)

To complicate this bewildering causal lineage, Oedipus – perhaps again like Ed – does not suffer *mere* bad luck: the incidents leading to Laius' murder play to a purpose, even if it is one of which Oedipus is unaware. He is unlucky, but he is also enacting out a series of events the *ends* of which are necessary, because they have been destined by the daemonic power of the gods. Perhaps the particular ways in which Oedipus' destiny is realized are individually random, but the outcomes to which they lead are not. "The pollution [of Thebes] was the effect of what he did – it was the dreadful curse he called upon himself in ignorance . . ." Williams notes, "but, of course, the daemonic was involved equally in the cause of what he did, because it was all fated before his birth" (Williams 1993: 60). The role of luck in the complicated causal web of tragedy is not straightforward; while nullifying the agential authority of one actor, it is often the agential vehicle of another. Similarly, *Mulholland Drive* introduces its own "daemonic" agents – puppeteers of the others' destinies – in the persons of the quarantined studio tyrant, Roque, and his henchman, the Cowboy.

Roque seems to be in control of the company making Adam Kesher's new film. He is off-limits – inaccessible and even invisible – to all the characters except (as we suppose) his butler. A glass wall blocks off his room, and he communicates via a telephone or a speaker system. A figure of mystery, he emerges from a shadowy darkness to address others, emphasizing his unnatural – almost supernatural – presence. When he does speak, he does so in ambiguous, single words that do not obviously answer the question posed to him; in this respect, his edicts are like the inscrutable utterance of the oracular figures in Greek tragedies, those mouthpieces of the gods who offered opaque glimpses of what was in store for the mortals whose lives they steer. Again like an Oracle's utterances, Roque's answers can be interpreted in almost any way the listener likes. This prompts us to question whether or not he can be held responsible for anything his company produces. If he didn't clearly order one thing or another, the subordinate interpreting the command is left to decide how it shall be enacted.[18]

An equally oracular figure in the film is the Cowboy; perhaps he is Roque's henchman, or perhaps he is the deity for whom Roque speaks. Either way, they are closely associated, and like Roque, the Cowboy emerges from darkness to give mystic, though more easily interpreted, commands. When he confronts Adam, he appears from and disappears back into the shadows, as if vanishing into an immaterial realm. Roque and the Cowboy attempt to instate Camilla Rhodes as the lead actress in Kesher's new film. This event not only throws Adam's life into complete disarray, disintegrating both his professional and marital arrangements, but places him in a classic, tragic dilemma: he must choose between his artistic integrity and his very life. It also initiates a central plot line in the second narrative, for it causes Diane to meet Camilla and thereby sets in motion the course of events leading to their violent deaths. The act of securing Camilla's role in Adam Kesher's film is thus not a mere manipulation of local outcomes but, ultimately, a gesture deciding who shall live and who shall die. In this respect, the Cowboy is an agent of theological proportions: a divine or supernatural intervention. This role is later confirmed when, in the film's second narrative he awakens Diane – or perhaps beckons her back from the dead: like the son of God restoring Lazarus, he calls to her to rise, and Diane is restored.

Roque and the Cowboy seem to be the only figures in *Mulholland Drive* who are properly in control of their destinies and able to effectively impose their wills on the world. They exercise this control, moreover, in ways that are inaccessible and unintelligible both to the other characters and to the viewer, and which defy ordinary causal laws. We are clearly invited to regard them as belonging on one side of fate – as deities that move the film's characters to action and leave them to suffer the consequences alone. Literally untouchable – Roque is physically shielded from the world, and the Cowboy seems to vanish into thin air – there is no way for their victims to hold them to account, nor exact punishment for the debacles they have ordered and orchestrated. Only their victims – Adam, Diane, and Camilla – suffer for their machinations.

The Cowboy acknowledges this himself during his meeting with Adam. He asks Adam whether or not he agrees that the course of a man's life is determined primarily "by his attitude." The Cowboy goes on to observe that if Adam agrees with this statement then he must not care about "living the good life." He implies that Adam can come along for the ride (meaning, it seems, not only that he can still direct *The Sylvia North Story* but that he will be allowed to survive) only if Adam fixes his attitude. In light of the film's concern with responsibility for actions beyond our control, this particular exchange is profoundly important: it is an open acknowledgement that the good life is not something we can sensibly strive for or bring about, for we have no direct control over whether or not we obtain it. Our task, rather, is to adopt an attitude of *passive compliance* toward what is presented to us; this is the only thing over which we have control.

A related thought is echoed in the character of Jimmy Katz, the actor, in response to Booker's criticism. Katz denies his responsibility for delivering a line too quickly, saying that all that he does is "react" to the other actor's delivery. He even proposes that such reacting is just what acting consists of: what an actor does is decided purely by the decisions of other actors – over whom he has no control. (It is worth noting that Lynch assigns this view to a professional *actor* – someone whose *raison d'être* is not to express his own nature, or to choose his actions, but to perform a scripted role – to generate the illusion of an agential self.) As with the Cowboy's advice to Adam, the prescription here is that one passively comply with what is given to one. But what can this mean, if *every* actor is merely reacting to every other? Jimmy's statement is surely ironic: after all, the woman auditioning is an actress who, by his own lights, can only be reacting to Jimmy. Thus, no one – or at least no actor – bears ultimate responsibility for how any line is delivered. Delivering a line, whether on a stage or in the theater of life, can never be more than adjusting one's reactions – one's "attitude." The only genuine agents are those who originate action: Roque and the Cowboy. Others can only "fix their attitudes" in response to them. And perhaps, if we react as required, we can get on the buggy.

Lynch offers a final reminder that our agency can be nullified by supernatural powers at the scene of Diane's suicide. We have reason to believe that Diane could, in principle, have been spared this end: in the first narrative, the mirror image of her body in bed shows no obvious cause of death. Moreover, she is driven to suicide by what seems to be an hallucination of her personal "Furies" – Irene and her companion, an elderly couple whom she met on her way to Hollywood. Even in the fantasy world Lynch constructs for *Mulholland Drive*, the appearances of these Furies are exceptionally odd. The couple, originally portrayed as both kindly and almost absurdly affectionate, occupy an enigmatic post in the film. We are introduced to them as a well-meaning elderly couple who have befriended Diane on the plane. After they part from her, however, we briefly glimpse them exchanging sinister and conspiratorial grins, casting into doubt the benign profile of moments earlier. In keeping with this, they take on a radically different mantle later in the film when they reappear as Furies – divine retribution for Diane's sin. (In this role, their bearing is not one of moral repudiation; as Furies – instruments of an amoral "eye for eye" justice – they instead terrorize Diane with maniacal laughter.) These are, Lynch suggests, enigmatic presences from another realm, playing with Diane's human susceptibility to the moral emotions.[19] The Furies act and Diane reacts, perversely holding herself to account as the agent of Camilla's death. She is driven to embrace death, that ultimate nullifier of personal choice and will.

What are we to make of these suggestions? What do they imply in the framework of the theoretical conception of identity and agency set out earlier? One might take them at face value, as signaling our inability to be agents at all. But this cannot be quite right: Adam Kesher, for instance, initially *resists* Roque's imperatives, and *protests* against his loss of authority over his work of art. He is, it seems, capable of doing more than deferring to fate's imperatives. In that respect he is a potential agent, possessed of a specific identity, and he thus confronts a dilemma which Jimmy Katz – a mere impersonator, or non-person – does not: he must choose between his agency and his well-being. (A first indication that his personal authority is under threat comes when, following his meeting with Roque's deputies, he returns home to find his wife in bed with another man.) We suggest that Lynch is here presenting a further source of discontinuity between choice and intention on the one hand, and our ability to enact these, on the other. Kesher, unlike Betty/Diane and Rita/Camilla, is not internally fractured; he has a stable direction, a valued project, a stated aim. (He is, after all, a *director*.) But the unity of agency requires more than a well-ordered psychology, just as a political state requires more than a well-ordered constitution: it also requires freedom from constraints. Hume held that we are free so long as we can act "as we will"; constraints to action prevent us from acting as we wish. Agency is not just a matter of possessing the requisite internal unity to will and will consistently, but the power to integrate one's willing with one's environment and to bring about states of the world: it is not only causal potential, but causal efficacy. If one's choices are doomed to be inefficacious – if the outcomes of one's actions are already otherwise determined – then one's agency is again fragmented, albeit in a different sense. Now the discontinuity emerges at a later point in the trajectory: the backward- and forward-looking, temporally extended process that constitutes agency is nullified by the intervention of overriding causal forces. Agency here is fractured not from within but from without, by distal interventions which leave the (would-be) agent suspended between his sense of himself as a locus of causality and a world in which his actions are futile, his choices utterly benign. Chance and the destinies designed by others together are our contemporary pantheon of gods: inscrutable, amoral, and omnipotent.

This idea was already implicit in the account proposed earlier of how the requirements of agency give rise to the idea of a persisting personal identity: from the subjective standpoint of practical action, we cannot but conceive of ourselves as the originators – the prime movers and shapers – of possible conditions of the world. This much is decided by the form of self-conscious, deliberative experience. At the same time, our best theoretical knowledge tells us that we cannot, in fact, be any such thing. Neither standpoint can be repudiated, and neither left behind; we stand in the space of possibilities in-between. In the world of Mulholland Drive, Kant's two standpoints – the practical standpoint of agency and the theoretical one of alien laws – do not deliver personal agency as a happy possibility; they rather condemn us to dream of it as an intelligible possibility which we can never realize. We know what it is, or would be, to exist as free agents, but necessity finally decides what we do.

Silencio

> The mind is a kind of theatre, where several perceptions successively make their appearance; pass, re-pass, glide away, and mingle in an infinite variety of postures and situations. There is properly no simplicity in it at one time,

nor identity in different. . . . nor have we the most distant notion of the place, where these scenes are represented, or of the materials, of which it is compos'd.

(Hume 1740, 253)

Suppose, as we have suggested, that the very idea of a person as a unique, individual entity is an idea derived from our awareness of ourselves as practical agents: an idea of ourselves as a unified locus of causality, an originator of action, persisting across different times and different places. (Perhaps this is part of what people mean when they speak, as Kant does, of a person as a special kind of entity meriting respect; it also has affinities with the theological notion of the soul.) This would be an idea of our individual identity grounded, at least in part, in what we are able to do. Now suppose further that we discover we do not do very much, if anything at all – that our agential powers are an illusion, and that the person who was purported to own them is an impotent conduit of alien influences, moving as they will. Is this Lynch's image of "Silencio," with which he ends *Mulholland Drive?*

In the Club Silencio there is no band; there is no orchestra; the sounds we hear issue from a tape. "Everything is an illusion," the stage magician tells his spectators. It is all recorded. The cast of Silencio are not genuine actors. They are not, themselves, the source of the sounds we hear: they merely pantomime in time with a pre-recorded track. It is a sinister, almost perverse, "show of agency" – a parody of what we ordinarily take ourselves to be. The dramatic culmination of the performance is Rebekah Del Rio's song. Her beautiful, impassioned performance is profoundly moving. Rita and Betty are overwhelmed; they weep together and hold one another in a moment of intense intimacy, hands clasped, tears mingling. It is unimaginable that Del Rio is not feeling and singing with every fiber of her soul. But there is no soul, no song, no Del Rio: she collapses, and the music carries on, exposing this climactic expression of humanity as an exercise in lip-sync and slick deception. The singer invoking such passionate response is not the charlatan on stage – Del Rio is not the singer; she is not even necessary for the song to continue; she is a shell without substance.

Silencio is a pre-recorded illusion, in which what seems to be happening in the present is in fact an echo of past events. The wider temporal logic of *Mulholland Drive* reinforces this symbol for the futility of human action. The film itself is sounds and images sewn together by a magician: the magician is Lynch. The intertwining of future and past, dream and reality, that structures *Mulholland Drive* suggests that we have little authority over who we are and what we do. The two narratives interact with each other in causally impossible ways: telephone calls placed in one narrative mysteriously reach phones in the second; *The Silvia North Story* has two different directors; and the same actresses win and lose the same parts by different means. The actresses' roles are gifted and taken by forces external to them. Recall Jimmy's theory of acting: actresses must only be reacting in their auditions; they must not be agents.

Hume notoriously argued that when he introspected, he did not find a self, but only a stream of perceptions. Perhaps, Lynch suggests, Hume was right, at least as regards the agential self. Our actions are often not our own. What we in fact are conflicts with what we think ourselves to be: we are not metaphysically unified agents or selves persisting, unbroken, through time. Unconscious aspects of character may steer our practical judgements, and conflicting elements of our subjective motivational sets can determine the course of our lives. These obscure loci of agency – not some discrete, independent, identifiable self – are all that we can point to in explanation of what we do and who we are. Blind luck and the bidding of those more powerful (or perhaps, only more lucky) than us, force our hands and prompt us to act in ways contrary to our hopes, desires, and plans. (A poorly aimed shot spoils the most calculated of professional hits; a misinterpreted command from Roque causes an entire life to unravel.) The agential self is suspended tenuously between these causal tracks: we exist as the forces that compel us to action, be they internal or external. Indeed, what we substantively are – our mode of existence – is nothing more than the point at which such forces converge; we delude ourselves into thinking that our actions *begin* with an independent, identifiable self – that we pre-exist such forces as an ultimate source, a first cause. While we imagine ourselves to be agents, to have a persistent identity, we are in truth nothing other than the theater in which these conflicting forces play out.

At the level of practical action, we wager that we can nonetheless make genuine choices and impose them on the world. Lynch suggests that this bet is poorly placed. We are not unified agents, metaphysically tied together as individual selves. Instead, we are the pantomiming actors on the Silencio stage: we act out the pre-recorded machinations of unconscious desires, the trappings of chance and destiny and the whims of the gods. We sit at the uncomfortable intersection of these forces – we just *are* the uncomfortable intersection of these forces.

The Greek tragedians articulated this sense of powerlessness in tales of supernatural divinities and their interventions in human affairs. We no longer include such entities in our everyday ontologies – we no longer imagine ourselves to be the marionettes of supernatural puppeteers. In that respect, of course, we may think of ourselves as "free" in a sense unavailable to our ancient ancestors. But perhaps part of Lynch's message is that no great gains attach to our alternative, modern self-conception. As Bernard Williams observes,

> When the world of supernatural necessities went away, this left human beings, to that extent, free; and when we become finally clear that a causal order, the possibility of explaining human desires and actions, is not itself a continuation of the old supernatural necessities, just because it has no purposive or preemptive character, then it will be finally clear that human beings are free. But this news is less exciting than it may sound. What human beings have . . . is metaphysical freedom. . . . Human beings are metaphysically free in the negative sense that there is nothing in the structure of the universe that denies their power to intend, to decide, to act, indeed to take and receive responsibility. . . . But metaphysical freedom is nothing – or at any rate, very little.
>
> (Williams 1993: 152)

Negative, metaphysical freedom from the supernatural threats of old makes it easier for us to imagine that we possess substantive, agential selves. We conceive of ourselves now as possessing the power to "intend, to decide, to act, . . . to take and receive responsibility," but these are, like Hume's perceptions, episodes occurring on an empty stage: metaphysical freedom leaves us with the absence, not the emergence, of a source of agency. This is why "nothing original" occurs on the Silencio stage: no agents exist to serve as origins, as first causes: everything that happens has its source not with the performers on stage, but with the tape they act out. What appears to be the conscious power of the performer has its sources outside of her, in sounds and images sewn together by a magician. Thus Del Rio's disappearance summons the components necessary to discovering Rita's identity – the mysterious box which holds the answer to the question of who she really is. At the moment the box and the key are brought together, Betty disappears, for the answer to that question is the end of her dream: Rita is nothing but a wishful fantasy. Perhaps it signals the end of one of our own dreams as well – a metaphysical dream of a unique, particular soul within, unifying all that we experience, think, feel, and do. The impassioned song on the Silencio stage is nothing but a stream of notes that proceeds from no one and expresses nothing. Are we, too, performers of scripts we do not author, illusory echoes of agency?

Notes

1   Compare Sophocles: Oedipus is informed that the pestilence in Thebes is owed to the unpunished slaying of Laius and that the murderer must be found. He responds to this news by demanding to be told, "Where is it to be found, this obscure trace of an ancient crime?" We, the spectators, can easily respond to his question, for we know the crime was his own; indeed, we are tempted to regard Oedipus – "that eager problem solver", as Williams says – with some slight disdain (1993: 58).

2   Countless hypothetical cases have been used to test our intuitions about synchronic identity: Can a single body house more than one agent or person? Can two bodies count as the same person, if they are psychologically identical? Which aspects of my psychology – memories, dispositions, temperament – are essential to deciding my identity?

3   Radden gives an interesting account of how we individuate persons in the context of dissociative identity disorder (formerly multiple personality) (1996: see especially 41, where criteria like these are given).

4   We are, clearly, subscribing to a psychological theory of personal identity. Such views take the continuity of psychological states as being necessary for the persistence of a person as that person through time. These views are typically in the lineage of Locke, and the great contemporary champion of such views is Parfit, who takes uniqueness and the holding of Relation-R – psychological connectedness/continuity with certain caveats – to be the conditions of personal identity (1987: 263). Psychological views of identity are not the only alternatives. Though we do not confront them here, various biological views of identity exist that posit the continuing existence of an organism as the primary condition of diachronic identity. As with psychological accounts, there are diverse formulations of such a view, but we will not discuss or consider such views here. For one prominent biological view of identity, see DeGrazia 2005. Again, we do not intend to discuss rival views of identity or thoroughly survey the terrain.

5   We do not intend to argue for this clam here. Parfit offers a sustained defense of it in *Reasons and Persons* (1987: see especially §86).

6 Are we avoiding the background question here of whether or not this practical self-conception is an illusion? Korsgaard follows Kant (and Strawson) in holding that this is a question we can only address theoretically; as agents, our practical natures must reject it. She comments, "We may regard ourselves as objects of theoretical understanding, natural phenomena whose behavior may be causally explained and predicted like any other. Or we may regard ourselves as agents, as the thinkers of our thoughts, and the originators of our actions. These two standpoints cannot be completely assimilated to each other, and the way we view ourselves when we occupy one can appear incongruous with the way we view ourselves when we occupy the other. As objects of theoretical study, we see ourselves as wholly determined by natural forces, the mere undergoers of our experiences. Yet as agents, we view ourselves as free and responsible, as the authors of our actions, and the leaders of our lives. This incongruity need not become contradiction, so long as we keep in mind that the two views of ourselves spring from two different relations in which we stand to our actions. When we look at our actions from the theoretical standpoint our concern is with their explanation and prediction. When we view them from the practical standpoint our concern is with their justification and choice. These two relations to our actions are equally legitimate, inescapable, and governed by reason, but they are separate" (Korsgaard 1989: 377–78).

7 Parfit argues that what matters in identity is just psychological continuity/connectedness (in terms of his Relation-R).

8 This choice of pseudonym is telling: Hayworth changed her hair color and her name in order to get cast as a leading lady. Also, the movie poster advertises *Gilda*, which features a dangerous love triangle.

9 The Iowa Gambling Task is used in experimental studies of decision-making. Subjects are presented with four (virtual) sets of cards, and invited to choose cards from decks for monetary reward. Some are "winning" decks and others are losers; healthy subjects typically tend to identify which is which over forty to fifty plays, and to prefer the winning decks. Many dysfunctional subjects – including autistics, psychopaths, and those with orbitofrontal damage – tend to persevere with the "bad" decks.

10 Even Adam is portrayed in contradictory ways in the two narratives as well. In the first, he is ineffectual and insecure. In the second, he is confident and successful.

11 This is tipped by Camilla's watchful glance at Diane, checking to see that her indiscreet betrayal has been noticed and has elicited its intended distress.

12 Rita, too, is an endearing if more unsettling character; in her amnesiac state she is spontaneous and uncalculating, vulnerable, and disarmingly affectionate and grateful.

13 The early scene with Dan and Herb ties together many of the film's thematic elements and preoccupations. Dan tells Herb of a dream he has had twice now, in which he is sitting in the very Winkie's in which they are currently

dining. At the end of a dream, he sees a man's face that is the source of all the terror he and Herb feel in the dream. He has brought Herb to this Winkie's to confront the dream and prove to himself that the man is not behind the restaurant as he is in the dream. They initiate a re-enactment of the dream, and in the end, a tramp appears behind the dumpster and frightens Dan to death – though it seems Herb has not seen the face.

14 This would, of course, entail that Rita is an idealized version of Camilla or a re-envisioning of Camilla, had she survived the hit that Diane ordered.

15 And yet when Betty is auditioning – in a scene about a forbidden affair – Watts plays Betty flawlessly, and the staff of the fictitious film is impressed with Betty's performance. Watts' performance in this scene stands in stark contrast to her portrayal of Betty in the rest of the film. Only during the audition does Betty's character show depth and complexity, subtle emotion. Only when the character is acting is Betty believable. She isn't really a person when she's being herself – she is more real when she's pretending; otherwise, she's just a caricature.

16 *Mulholland Drive* (2001) is not the only of Lynch's pieces to take up the issue of one body housing two radically conflicting agential drives. In *Twin Peaks* (1990–91) Leland Palmer is possessed by Bob the spirit of evil and murders his daughter – Bob will ultimately go on to possess Agent Cooper as well. Both Leland's and Cooper's bodies become host to two persons – Bob is a person unto himself that can exist whether he is possessing someone or not. In *Twin Peaks* and *Twin Peaks: Fire Walk with Me* (1992), Laura Palmer is an oddly schizoid character: she is the popular, beautiful homecoming queen; but she is also a drug-addicted prostitute. This deep internal conflict within a character is one aspect of Lynch's concern across his corpus with the difference between appearance and reality.

17 At the same time, Joe cannot be absolved of responsibility. He may be luck's unwitting accomplice, but he is still a killer and will presumably murder again; indeed, it is revealed in other scenes that Diane has engaged him to track down Camilla. From one point of view, arbitrary chance led him to kill two innocents; from another perspective, these murders issue from the fact that Joe *is* a murderer: had he not killed Ed, no amount of bad luck would have made him the instrument of the others' deaths.

18 Bob, the director at Betty's audition, speaks in similarly oblique and ambiguous terms.

19 *Mulholland Drive* is not the only of Lynch's works presenting this dynamic. In *Twin Peaks*, Leland may be possessed by Bob when he kills Laura and Maddy, but he invited Bob in as a child – so his own agency is connected to these foreign acts. In *Blue Velvet* (1986), Jeffrey Beaumont is pulled into a world of corruption, drugs, and violence, but his own curiosity and sexual desire for Dorothy Vallens led him there. In the context of agential nullification, Lynch shows us that we are all players in a tragedy. Our agency and ability to act is not determined by our choices alone. Though aspects of our characters –

particularly the darker aspects – motivate us, our options are constrained by external, often mysterious and ineffable, forces that dictate what we may or may not pursue. Tragedy is, for Lynch, a given condition of human agency.

References

DeGrazia, D. (2005) *Human Identity and Bioethics*, Cambridge: Cambridge University Press.

Gerrans, P. and J. Kennett (2010) "Neurosentimentalism and Moral Agency," *Mind* 119: 585–614.

Holbach, P. H. T., baron d' (1770) "The Illusion of Free Will" from *The System of Nature*; page reference is to the reprint in D. Kolak and R. Martin (eds), *The Experience of Philosophy*, 5th edn (Oxford: Oxford University Press, 2002).

Hume, D. (1740/1978) *A Treatise of Human Nature*, ed. L. A. Selby-Bigge and P. H. Nidditch, 2nd edn, New York: Oxford University Press.

Korsgaard, C. (1989) "Personal Identity and the Unity of Agency: A Kantian Response to Parfit," *Philosophy & Public Affairs* 18: 101–32; page references are to the repr. in C. Korsgaard, *Creating the Kingdom of Ends* (New York: Cambridge University Press, 1996), pp. 363–97.

Lynch, D. (dir.) (1986) *Blue Velvet*, perf. Kyle MacLachlan and Isabella Rossellini, screenplay by David Lynch, Wilmington, NC: De Laurentiis Entertainment Group.

—— (dir.) (1990–91) *Twin Peaks*, created by David Lynch and Mark Frost, perf. Sheryl Lee, Ray Wise, and Kyle MacLachlan, New York: American Broadcasting Company.

—— (dir.) (1992) *Twin Peaks: Fire Walk with Me*, perf. Sheryl Lee, Ray Wise and Kyle MacLachlan, screenplay by David Lynch and Robert Engels, Los Angeles, CA: New Line Cinema.

—— (dir.) (2001) *Mulholland Drive*, perf. Naomi Watts, Laura Elena Harring, and Justin Theroux, screenplay by David Lynch, Universal City, CA: Universal Studios.

Parfit, D. (1987) *Reasons and Persons*, Oxford: Oxford University Press.

Radden, J. (1996) *Divided Minds and Successive Selves: Ethical Issues in Disorders of Identity and Personality*, Cambridge, MA: MIT Press.

Vernant, J. and P. Vidal-Naquet (1981) *Tragedy and Myth in Ancient Greece*, vol. 1, trans. J. Loyd, Brighton: Harvester Press.

Williams, B. A. O. (1993) *Shame and Necessity*, Berkeley, CA: University of California Press.

Chapter 3

Alan Nelson

COWBOY RULES:

MULHOLLAND DRIVE, KAFKA, AND ILLUSORY FREEDOM

A N   A S P I R I N G   A C T R E S S   A R R I V E S   in Los Angeles. It is sunny and warm. On the drive north from the airport the Hollywood sign overlooks the city from the hills that have Mulholland Dr. snaking along their crest. She has left behind her life in Deep River, Ontario, to pursue a new one with better work, better pay, better lovers and friends, better weather – everything better. This seems reasonable; her aunt made a good life for herself in the movie industry. Moreover, Diane Selwyn is young, attractive, and full of energy and optimism. She is a character in Mulholland Drive, a film by David Lynch, so we already know that events will not unfold according to her plan. Although she initially makes some of the conventionally correct moves, it seems that inexorable forces are positioned to thwart her. Her position progressively deteriorates and things end very badly for her.

K., a land surveyor by trade, arrives in the village. He is a character in The Castle, a novel by Franz Kafka, so it is natural that he arrives in snow and darkness. The village is overlooked by a castle on the hill, but "There was no sign of the Castle hill, fog and darkness surrounded it, not even the faintest gleam of light suggested the large Castle."[1] Although this much is a mirror image of Diane's arrival, the rest of K.'s situation is very similar. He has left behind his homeland, wife and child, with high hopes for a surveying job he expects to take up in the village. K. is older and seemingly more accomplished than Diane. He works with two assistants who manage his surveying equipment although, ominously, they seem to have lost their way to the village. Like Diane's efforts, K.'s will be thwarted and his position progressively deteriorates. Recalling the fate of the similarly named Joseph K. in Kafka's The Trial, it is easy to imagine that K. will meet an end very similar to Diane's. One senses that it is only in virtue of Kafka's failing to finish the novel that K. is spared the end that is shared by Diane and Joseph K.

Lynch's films often explore much the same ground as Kafka's writings; this is obvious from their content as much as Lynch's own statements about Kafka.[2] Mulholland Drive is a strong case in point. In this essay I shall try to show how Kafka's The Castle, in particular, eerily parallels this great film in significant ways. Kafka's novels feature stifling, error-prone bureaucracies that are nevertheless generally accorded respect, or even veneration. His protagonists are victimized, apparently by mistake, and are frustrated in their attempts to seek redress. They are ostensibly free to do as they please. K. is not being held in the village against his will; he is at liberty to leave and is even encouraged to do so. And in The Trial, it appears that Joseph K. need not work to clear the mysterious charge against him. Were he to carry on as usual, it seems that the verdict in his case can be indefinitely postponed. In each case, however, the freedom is illusory. Both of the K.s are inevitably ruined by their encounters with the veiled powers that be.

Kafkaesque themes abound in most of Lynch's work. One is the juxtaposition of the mundane and supernatural found in Lost Highway and Twin Peaks, and another is the revelation of the sinister underbelly of the apparently wholesome that is prominent in Blue Velvet. One could go on, but it is interesting that Kafka's thematic conflict between murky power structures and the individual is not so clearly on display in the aforementioned films. Mulholland Drive, in contrast, foregrounds this opposition. For example, we see it clearly in the power that Mr Roque weirdly displays over the production of the film that Adam Kesher plans to direct. When the latter first spurns the directive, "This is the girl," Mr Roque transmits the message to his henchmen to "shut the whole thing down" in an almost telepathic way. Mr Roque is not directly accessible, not even to the Castiglianes who appear to be his main operatives. Instead, he greets audiences from behind a large glass (probably bulletproof) window. Adam's subsequent encounter with the Cowboy is similar. Although this time the relationship is adversarial, the transmission of Mr

Roque's power (or perhaps the power of associated forces) through the Cowboy is decidedly surreal. These events concerning Adam are, admittedly, a sequence in Diane's dream given the interpretation I favor. Nevertheless, they surely represent the way she experiences her own life as being controlled. At this point a little needs to be said about the general kind of interpretation of the film's structure that I shall be assuming.

It will be best to keep this structure minimal so that what I say might still be of interest when the reader's own interpretation is applied. I begin by assuming that most of the events depicted in the film are dreamed by Diane Selwyn. Diane dreams events in which her life in LA is recast as experienced by Betty Elms. The main characters in the dream are drawn from Diane's real life. With the important exception of Camilla Rhodes, they mostly retain their names and principal aspects of their real personalities. Rita is the dream version of Camilla, while a new Camilla in the dream plays only a minor role. Rita and the director, Adam Kesher, sometimes represent Diane's own perspectives or perhaps even her other personas. Diane awakens toward the end of the film, whereupon we view some flashbacks of her real life. Especially significant is a party at Adam's house to which the real Camilla has invited her. At this party, it is announced that Camilla (revealed in flashbacks to have been a lover of Diane's) and Adam are to be married. Despondent and angry, Diane orders a hit on Camilla and finally commits suicide in her apartment on Sierra Bonita. I do not claim that this kind of interpretation is the best possible, or even that the events in the film are best understood as interpretable as forming a coherent, linear narrative. It does, however, bring the themes I wish to discuss clearly to the fore.

The plot of Kafka's *The Castle*, while consistently bizarre, is free of the convolutions of *Mulholland Drive*. Again, a brief summary of the plot is in order. K. (this name, more minimal than even that of Joseph K. in *The Trial*, is the only one given) has come to the village controlled from what the inhabitants call the "Castle." Again, no name is given; I'll simply refer to it as "the village." The Castle is really just a complex of small, unimpressive buildings with one tower, but it is located on a hill and very difficult to access. K. plans to take up a position he has been offered as a surveyor. After his arrival, a courier delivers to K. a letter informing that there is, in fact, no post for him as a surveyor and that he should report to the village Chairman for a temporary reassignment while the Castle bureaucracy will (perhaps) re-evaluate the situation. This turns out to be a demeaning job as the custodian of the schoolhouse. There is no salary, but one of the perks of this job is that he can sleep in a classroom provided that he clears out each morning before the children arrive. K. is determined to appeal straightaway to officials in the Castle to rectify his situation. The Castle is, however, strangely inaccessible to visitors or even to messages. The oddly laid out roads are covered in deep snow and conveyance by sleigh is not to be had. Kafka's narrative covers just a few days during which K. attempts to use villagers and minor officials for some sadly indirect connections to officials from the Castle. Kafka left the novel unfinished, but he is said to have projected a conclusion in which K. hears on his deathbed that he will be able to continue to live and work in the village on a provisional basis.[3]

This essay examines three tightly intertwined threads in the lives of Diane Selwyn and K. that reflect their parallel struggles against dominating forces. One of these threads is about geographical displacement; both characters experience disruptive dislocations. A second thread follows instability in amorous relationships, and the third tracks identities as they are expressed by profession and occupation. Seeing how Lynch and Kafka weave these strands together will provide the basis for some ruminations about human freedom.

This essay began in the same way as the stories of Diane and K., with their leaving their established homes for entirely new environments. One way to narrate almost the entire story of *The Castle* would be to trace K.'s physical displacements as they are connected with the frustration of his efforts to integrate himself into the economy and social structure of the village. One must look a little closer, but only a little, to find similar displacements in *Mulholland Drive*. Unlike Diane, who finally settles into her second apartment on Sierra Bonita and dies there, K. experiences a series of displacements, evictions really, that is never resolved. Trudging through the deep snow after crossing the boundary into the village and seeking respite, he tumbles into the Bridge Inn. What could be more appropriate for a traveller and new resident of the village arriving at night seeking temporary lodging? The innkeeper is, however, "confused" by his arrival and can manage only a straw mat on the floor of the taproom for his new visitor. The exhausted K. falls asleep, but he is to have no peace on the floor. He is soon awakened by a man who identifies himself as the son of a steward in the Castle. This man attempts to eject K. from the inn because K. apparently lacks the required Castle clearance. K. firmly asserts himself (his manner might even be described as "smart-alecky" – more on this later) causing the official's son to telephone the Castle. A return call from the Castle dictates a reassessment that enables K. to stay – but only temporarily – at the inn. This arrangement is plainly unstable and cannot last.

In Diane's dream, Betty's arrival in LA is initially more promising than K.'s first encounter with the villagers, although the strange laughter of the old couple (parents or grandparents?) gives us pause. We later learn that the same is true of Diane's real arrival. Although things go more smoothly for Betty than for K., she is in for a bigger initial surprise. Upon entering her aunt's apartment she finds the shower occupied by the naked, amnesiac Rita. And Rita herself has survived both a car wreck and murder attempt to scramble down from Mulholland Dr. to the refuge of Aunt Ruth's West Hollywood apartment. For Betty, her aunt's apartment is an enchanting base of operations, but for Rita it is a temporary safe haven from the unknown forces that are still menacingly pursuing her. Betty comes to see matters that way as well.[4] Betty now has two missions to accomplish: audition for a role in a Hollywood production, and help Rita by discovering her identity. K. is also on a mission. After spending the night on the floor (bothered only slightly by some rats) he sets off for the Castle. Before long, the trudge through the snow exhausts him. (Oddly enough, the villagers seem to move quite freely through the snow.) By throwing a snowball into a village house, he manages to invite himself inside for a rest. Despite the bustle inside the house, K. falls asleep. After awakening, he indiscreetly approaches a woman who purports to be from the Castle, whereupon he is brusquely pulled to the door by two men. Next in this sequence, he receives the aforementioned letter by a messenger named Barnabas, which leads to his being in the messenger's cottage with his family. He is invited to spend the night here; Barnabas's sister, Olga, seems especially interested in K. and keen on his staying. But K. spurns this offer in favor of attempting to find a place at the village's other inn, the Gentleman's Inn, which is exclusively for Castle officials.

Surely enough the innkeeper at this establishment cites regulations and does not permit K. so much as a spot on the floor in the taproom like the spot he enjoyed the first night at the Bridge Inn. At the instigation of Frieda the barmaid at the Gentleman's Inn, however, he spends the night hidden with her on the floor behind the bar. It is hard to say which is more surprising – their having sex in puddles of spilled beer, or their somehow being engaged to be married by the next morning. The reader is not prepared for either. Frieda abandons her job as barmaid and the couple head back to K.'s Castle-approved garret at the Bridge Inn. This is a good place to interrupt the litany of K.'s upheavals by shifting back to *Mulholland Drive*. Many of the corresponding threats to Diane's actual residence in LA can be seen as projected onto the dream version of Adam Kesher. The real Adam lives in a house on Mulholland Dr. with his mother, Coco. It appears to be the same location at which the dream Adam initially lives with his wife. But in the dream, Adam suffers a series of dislocations that eerily parallel K.'s.

Things begin to go wrong for Adam in a meeting about the production of his upcoming film project. The shady Castigliane brothers announce that Adam must cast Camilla Rhodes (i.e. the dream version thereof) in the lead. He flatly refuses. Storming out of the meeting, he smashes the windshield of the Castigliane's ride with a golf club before setting off in his Porsche for his house on Mulholland Dr. As he will discover, powerful forces have "shut everything down" and he is effectively locked out of the studio. Adam arrives home planning to collect himself but instead finds his wife, Lorraine, in bed with the pool man. "What the hell are you even doing here?," she demands from the bed. He retaliates by dumping paint into her jewelry box and they begin to wrestle. Gene, the pool man, intervenes by slugging Adam. Lorraine instructs Gene to throw him out and Adam gets the bum's rush onto the driveway. He gets back into his car and repairs downtown to the seedy Park Hotel, a modern-day equivalent of Kafka's Bridge Inn. A good thing, too, because a thug soon shows up looking for him at his house. Soon after arriving at the Park Hotel, Adam, like K. receives bad news from the innkeeper. Powerful, nearly omniscient,[5] bureaucrats have somehow tracked him there and, more ominously, have frozen his bank accounts leaving him with only a wallet of cash.

Adam phones his secretary who confirms that he is "broke" (despite his having been wealthy a few hours ago). This means that even his lodgings at the Park Hotel are insecure; his only real option is to agree to a meeting that the Cowboy has suggested to his secretary, Cynthia. It is true that Cynthia offers to put Adam up, but he cannot be deflected from confronting the power that is dominating him. Cynthia tells him, "You don't know what you're missing," but Adam is unmoved by his messenger's entreaty, just as K. was unmoved by the invitation to stay with Olga, his messenger's sister. The encounter with the Cowboy will be discussed below, but now it can be noted that by dutifully following the Cowboy's instructions, Adam is reinstated as director of the film and presumably gets his entire life back on track. This contrasts sharply with what happens to Diane and to K.

We left K. back at the Bridge Inn with his new fiancée, Frieda. K. next sets off for the house of the village's Chairman as he was instructed to do in the letter he received. He learns there that there is no job in the village for a surveyor; his initial summons was the result of some miscommunication between the village and the Castle. The Chairman arranges a substitute post for him: janitor at the schoolhouse. The job offers no salary (!), but K. and Frieda will be permitted to sleep on a straw mattress in one of the classrooms provided that they clear out every morning before the schoolchildren arrive. K. immediately tells his prospective boss the school teacher the offer is rejected. K. prefers being temporarily ensconced in the maids' unsavory space in Bridge Inn's attic to the proposed lodgings. He figures that will be best for focusing on asserting his rights at the Castle. Nevertheless, Frieda presses on him the need to accept the job offer after all. The reason is that K.'s insistence on approaching Castle officials as directly as possible has angered one of the innkeepers at the Bridge Inn. K. is no longer welcome there so he must move. It is noteworthy that Coco, Betty's "innkeeper" at her aunt's apartment, while disapproving of Betty's association with Rita, remains supportive of Betty's effort to find an acting job.

The very first night in the schoolhouse, K. discovers that there is no heat despite the frigid winter weather, so he breaks into the woodshed to appropriate some firewood. The final upshot of that misdeed is that his employment, and lodging, is terminated; he and Frieda are ordered out. K. refuses to accept the termination, but as things turn out, he does not spend another night in the schoolhouse anyway. The next night is spent back at the Gentleman's Inn standing around waiting for an interview with a Castle official. The exhausted K. eventually takes a snooze in a guest room at the foot of a lesser official's bed during a discourse by the latter about Castle culture. (While drowsing, K. misses a possibility of making an inroad at the Castle.) After waking, K. surreptitiously hangs out in the corridor containing the Gentleman's rooms (against regulations, needless to say). Finally his trespass becomes intolerable, alarms ring out, and the innkeeper hustles K. out of the proscribed corridor. At first it seems K.'s pathetic request to sleep on a board laid over two barrels will be denied and that K. will be thrown out into the snow and predawn darkness.

> Being driven away from here seemed to him a misfortune that surpassed everything he has experienced up to now. That must not be allowed to happen, even if the landlord[6] and landlady were to be united against him. K. lay in wait, doubled up on the barrel, watching the two of them.
>
> (pp. 286–87)

But the innkeeper relents, perceiving that K. is still so sleepy he can hardly stand up. When he awakens from this makeshift bed, now in his fifth full day in the village, he is engaged in an exchange with Frieda's replacement as the Gentleman's Inn barmaid. She is Pepi, now promoted from chambermaid. She eventually proposes to K. another ghastly housing arrangement. He can stay in a room with her and two other chambermaids on the condition that he do some of their work, take their advice, and keep the arrangement secret because it is, of course, contrary to regulations. K. appears on the point of accepting the offer (because he is desperate? because he wants to be near the officials in this inn?), when they are interrupted by an innkeeper. She requires that they leave Pepi so that she can scold him about a remark K. had made about her dress before falling asleep. We have finally arrived at the last in the series of upheavals K. endures. K. is physically pulled away from the Gentleman's Inn by a coachman named Gerstäcker who thinks that K. can assist his own petition to the Castle. Gerstäcker proposes that K. accept food and lodging with him and his mother in their cottage in return for helping with the horses. K. seems to prefer this to Pepi's suggested arrangement and returns with Gerstäcker to his cottage. With K. apparently thus reduced to the status of stable boy, the novel abruptly ends unfinished.

While K.'s outrageous peregrinations through the village exceed Adam Kesher's appreciable discomfiture, Lynch nevertheless creates a similar atmosphere of alienation from home, and from place more generally. Rita's displacement has also been noted. Viewing *Mulholland Drive* one is also invited to speculate about Diane's real situation. Like K., she has chosen to leave her home for better prospects. One can see the logic in using Aunt Ruth's inheritance to attempt to follow in her footsteps in Hollywood. But she might have used it for college or to set herself up in Deep River, Ontario. Might there also be something sinister in Deep River that she hopes to escape? That would certainly be very Lynchian. For that matter, Kafka never explains why K., presumably a successful surveyor, should leave wife, child, and home for a long (permanent?) stay in the village overlooked by the Castle. There is also the mysterious business of Diane's having traded apartments with a neighbor in the Sierra Bonita complex. We do not know whether this is because she was trying to avoid some people (detectives? the Cowboy?) or whether it was, perhaps, due to some unpleasantness with a room-mate (Camilla?). Moreover, the fact that Diane dreams Adam into the sleazy Park Hotel suggests that she herself spent some time in that flophouse – perhaps before she earned enough to keep the apartment at Sierra Bonita.[7] Finally, when Betty and Rita flee in horror from the Sierra Bonita apartment, it is surely significant that it is Diane's real apartment, the one in which she is currently dreaming, that is so terrifying. Combined complications in romantic relationships and housing are evidently pervasive in both *Mulholland Drive* and *The Castle*.

None of the foregoing can be sharply separated from the love lives of the characters. Even if Diane's apartment switch at Sierra Bonita was not driven by her difficult split with Camilla, Adam's difficulties definitely include his wife's affair with the pool man (and perhaps he has had one with Cynthia – we can only speculate about how close they are). K.'s romantic entanglements are even more scrambled. He has left his wife (or has he abandoned her?) and becomes engaged to Frieda. On the day that he leaves Frieda in the schoolhouse, she feels abandoned and suspects that he is being unfaithful to her with Olga, the sister of Barnabas the messenger. Frieda abruptly leaves K., takes up with an odious villager, and is poised to be reinstated as barmaid at the Gentleman's Inn. It has already been noted that Frieda's replacement as barmaid, Pepi, has offered to lodge K. in her room with the two chambermaids who are her room-mates. That proposition has palpable sexual overtones. K. seems to have accepted that offer until he is waylaid by Gerstäcker and taken to his cottage instead.

Yet another manifestation of the subjection to power suffered by Diane and K. is the frustration of their ability to find meaningful employment.

K. never gets anywhere near doing any surveying. There is, in fact, no surveying to be done anywhere in the village; his training is worthless. The message he received summoning him to the village was the result of an error at the Castle. Once in the village he rapidly transitions from potential surveyor (married) to school janitor (engaged to be married) to potential chambermaid's assistant (and male concubine) to stable boy (and once again married?). Ironically, there is another sense in which K.'s present occupations and his prospects for the future are entirely stable. All of the transitions are merely notional. His real job, the one that occupies his thought and his time, is continually attempting to engage the Castle bureaucracy. Even his relationship with his fiancée is colored by the chance that she can be utilized in his quest for official recognition because she is the former mistress of a bureaucrat with a high position in the Castle. We understand that as long as K. stays in the village, the only fixed point in his existence will be his struggle for security. Neither his home, his relationships, his job, nor his very identity will be secured.

In *Mulholland Drive* we learn that Diane had a few small parts in films. How did she support herself? The inheritance from her aunt would not last long in Los Angeles. Perhaps she had been a waitress at Winkie's like the woman with the "Betty" name tag? We might also surmise that as an aspiring actress with very limited success she had become familiar with the casting couch. It is possible that this suggestion is confirmed by the presence of the Cowboy and the notice that one of the Castiglianes takes her at Adam and Camilla's engagement party. The Cowboy, moreover, seems to have access to her apartment; we see him open the door ("Hey, pretty girl, time to wake up!") and in her dream we see a cowboy hat hanging in Aunt Ruth's bedroom.[8] Furthermore, since Diane probably spent time in the Park Hotel, she might well have been exploited in even more degrading ways. In Diane's dream, Betty juggles the roles of aspiring actress and, as she takes up Rita's cause, guardian and detective as well. Diane's anxiety concerning employment is further reflected in her dream as Adam is threatened with the loss of his job and identity while Rita has entirely lost hers.

So far we have looked at how both Lynch and Kafka present us with characters that are unsettled in multiple dimensions. Their livelihoods, personal relationships, and even the spaces they are allowed to occupy are ephemeral. One way of drawing these together emerges in the pivotal scene in which Adam meets the Cowboy. Here, high above the city, Adam gets the kind of direct, effective guidance that K. is unable to get from the Castle. It is undeniable that the Cowboy's presentation is creepy and weird and Adam is shaken by it, but he leaves the corral with a clear picture of what he must do.

Adam asks what is on the Cowboy's mind, and he replies with the maxim, "a man's attitude goes some ways to the way his life will be." He wants to know whether Adam agrees. Adam says "Sure," but that is excessively glib for the Cowboy. He demands that the pronouncement be repeated and Adam complies by offering this translation of the garbled statement: "A man's attitude determines to a large extent how his life will be." Now the Cowboy enjoins him to think about it.

> Adam: OK, I'm thinking.
> Cowboy: No, you're not thinkin'. You're too busy bein' a smart aleck to be thinkin'. Now I want you to think and stop bein' a smart aleck. Can you try that for me?
> Adam: Look, where's this going? What do you want me to do?
> Cowboy: There's sometimes a buggy. How many drivers does a buggy have?
> Adam: One.
> Cowboy: So let's just say I'm drivin' this buggy and if you fix your attitude, you can ride along with me.

The Cowboy has implicitly insisted on the original statement of the maxim in terms of *ways*. Adam can be a passenger in the Cowboy's buggy while he drives it along the *way* to the good life. But if Adam attempts to seize the reins and drive the buggy himself, it will go the wrong *way* – the wrong way for someone who "care[s] about the good life." The Cowboy then offers a concrete instance of his general rule. Adam must say "This is the girl" after the actress the Castiglianes indicated has completed her audition.

The Cowboy's characterizing Adam's behavior at their meeting in the corral as "smart-alecky" might seem unfair – what else could Adam have said? But there is considerable justice in his evaluation of his overall attitude. Adam's initial refusal to accept that "this is the girl" and smashing the Castiglianes' windshield sharply resisted the order imposed by the Hollywood powers. From the Cowboy's perspective this *is* smart-alecky. Later we see that Adam has returned to the set of his film, once again enjoying the good life. Now he is following the Cowboy's rules. The Cowboy is driving the buggy and Adam is along for the ride. This all takes place in Diane's dream, but the situation of the real Adam is not so different.[9] We see him at the party in his house on Mulholland Dr. having successfully negotiated a divorce ("I got the pool, she got the pool man"), and happily contemplating marriage to Camilla. In addition to Diane, the party's guests include the Cowboy and a Castigliane. The real Adam's happiness and the price he has paid are both clear. He has himself become a minor figure in the power structure.

Before examining how Diane's situation is illuminated by what happens between Adam and the Cowboy, a comparison with K. is in order. One striking feature of his personality is that he is relentlessly "smart-alecky": self-assertive, curt to the point of rudeness, and dismissive of the concerns of the villagers. K. is driving his own buggy and his way leads nowhere good. That is a metaphor; it is impossible to get a buggy ride to the Castle. K. never has an encounter with Castle functionaries anything like the dream Adam's with the Cowboy. The messages K. receives are indirect and cryptic as opposed to the Cowboy's explicit instructions. It does appear, however, that he could have stayed in the attic of the Bridge Inn or have been the schoolhouse janitor indefinitely. And Frieda expressed a strong desire to leave the village with him and head to France or Spain. These possibilities gave K. some measure of freedom to avoid his struggle with the Castle.

Is Diane also a smart aleck resisting the forces that would oppress her? The dreamed Betty persona is an adventurous risk-taker. She accepts Camilla into her aunt's house and deceives her "innkeeper" about it. She undertakes some potentially dangerous sleuthing, including breaking and entering at Sierra Bonita. In her audition she takes an audacious chance with her interpretation. Finally, Betty boldly enters Club Silencio with Rita, a confrontation with mysterious power that leads to the end of the dream. Betty's free activity is no more successful than K.'s. Diane Selwyn is more of a conformist than Betty. She takes the conventional route for someone trying to break into acting in Hollywood, but not successful in her one big chance at an audition. That audition was the occasion of her meeting the real Camilla and while her career sputters, she derives happiness for a while from their romantic relationship.

Diane does something highly subversive only when it is too late. After Camilla has dumped her to marry Adam and apparently taken another woman as lover, Diane repudiates her entire existence in Hollywood by having Camilla killed. Had she been able to stand it, Diane might have conformed to the new situation and, perhaps, tried to keep alive her acting career by ingratiating herself with the new couple. Instead, she sets in motion the plan for deadly revenge. The police do not find her (unless it is they who insistently knock on her door at the very end), but order is restored. Diane's gesture against Hollywood's power structure and her place in it is punished by her emotional and mental collapse and suicide. Just as K. could have accepted a reduced position in the village or left altogether for his old home or even France, Diane seems to have had options. She could have accepted a reduced position in Camilla's circle, based on friendship instead of love. For that matter, no explicit reason is given for why she should not start to take college classes, or return to Deep River, Ontario.

All of this might suggest that Lynch and Kafka are both illustrating the idea that resistance is futile. If, like the dreamed Adam, one wants the good life or a semblance of it, one should follow the Cowboy's (or the Castle's) rules and not try for more. One can freely choose to attain the good life by being a passenger in the Cowboy's buggy, but strict compliance is required – no back-seat driving. This assessment, however, is too simple. The Adam we see in Diane's dream *begins* in a privileged position. His smart-alecking violates the Cowboy's rules; following them *restores* his position in the order. In real life, too, Adam is already a part of the power structure, though probably a minor one. Camilla is, as well, by the time of her engagement to Adam, and perhaps even before that. It seems likely that Diane was never sufficiently significant to draw the explicit enforcement mechanisms of the Hollywood power structure. Implicit force suffices to keep the less fortunate, such as she, quiet in the back seat of the buggy.

Diane and K. begin their stories in positions of weakness. Diane mostly follows the rules until she hits bottom and disastrously retaliates. K. is determined to resist the obstacles placed before him, but he makes no progress and even loses ground. Could either of them have done better? We can straightaway rule out their returning "home." There is never so much as a hint that considers this option which is, in the abstract, clearly available. The unavoidable conclusion is that something even worse –

something that cannot be faced – awaits them in their old hometowns.[10] Once leaving home, Diane's only chance for the good life is in Los Angeles, and K.'s is in the Castle's village. Nor does it seem that Diane could have done more to exploit her tenuous Hollywood connections, namely the career of her deceased aunt and her relationship with Camilla, a successful actress. It is interesting that in Diane's dream, the roles are reversed and Rita is dependent on Betty, but Betty is ultimately unable to resolve either Rita's situation or her own. It is even more obvious that K. takes every opportunity to make use of his own feeble connections. And it is correspondingly interesting that every non-Castle person K. attempts to exploit is probably simultaneously trying to exploit him. For example, one might think that K.'s motive for beginning the relationship with Frieda is to stake a claim to belonging in the village. But Pepi, Frieda's temporary replacement as barmaid, interprets Frieda's motive to be the strengthening of her relationship with the important Castle official whose mistress she was before her attachment to K. This man frequents the Gentleman's Inn. And, in fact, we learn that the Castle does want her returned to the Gentleman's Inn. Frieda leaves K. to take up her old position with Castle approval. Even in retrospect, there is no more effective course of action to recommend to either Diane or K.

Diane and K. appear to enjoy considerable freedom. But it is hollow; their actions have no effect on the forces that stultify them. There is a passage in The Castle that crystallizes K.'s predicament. After waiting for a long time in a freezing courtyard in a failed attempt to waylay a Castle official, K. felt,

> . . . as if he were freer than ever and could wait as long as he wanted here in this place where he was generally not allowed, and as if he had fought for this freedom for himself in a manner nobody else could have done and as if nobody could touch him or drive him away, or even speak to him, yet – and this conviction was at least equally strong – as if there were nothing more senseless, nothing more desperate, than this freedom, this waiting, this invulnerability.
> (p. 106)

Diane's final desperate gesture of autonomy is effective, but self-destructive. Lynch's crystallization of Diane's predicament is briefer, but as eloquent as Kafka's: Silencio!

Notes

1 F. Kafka, *The Castle*, trans. Mark Harman (New York: Schocken Books, 1998), p. 1. All page references are to this edition, unless otherwise noted.

2 "The one artist that I feel could be my brother – and I almost don't like saying it because the reaction is always, 'Yes, you and everybody else' – is Franz Kafka. I really dig him a lot. Some of his things are the most thrilling combos of words I have ever, ever, ever read. If Kafka wrote a crime picture, I'd be there. I'd like to direct that for sure." (David Lynch, from an interview by David Chute conducted at the Bob's Big Boy, corner of Wilshire and Highland, June 1986). Published in *Film Comment* (September/October 1986), p. 34.

3 Publisher's note p. vi, *The Castle* (New York: Alfred A. Knopf, 1968).

4 The forces are unknown to both women. We, on the other hand, hear Mr Roque complain that "the girl is still missing" and see the hit man trying to track her on the streets. We also learn later that Diane is a person of interest in a murder investigation.

5 Cookie seems sympathetic to Adam's plight, citing his "duty" to inform him. But perhaps he also has duties to those seeking to coerce Adam.

6 I have been translating *Wirt* and *Wirtin* in Kafka's German as "innkeeper."

7 Another strong clue that Diane has been in the Park Hotel is that a man appearing on the stage at Club Silencio bears a striking resemblance to Cookie. Diane must have seen him at least once to be able to dream that.

8 This placement of the cowboy hat also indicates how controlling forces penetrate even the place that, for Betty, epitomizes the glamor and promise of Hollywood.

9 The main difference seems to be that in the dream Adam instinctively connects with Betty but is prevented from pursuing the connection because of the Cowboy's rules. The real Adam takes little notice of Diane who is a mere extra in his film.

10 Evidence for this might be drawn from Lynch's use of the old couple who are seen with Diane at the jitterbug contest and at her arrival in LA. They seem to represent her connection with home in Deep River. But at the end they are seen emerging from the blue box held by the monster behind Winkie's and finally terrorizing Diane in her apartment to the point where she shoots herself.

Chapter 4

Zina Giannopoulou

MULHOLLAND DRIVE AND CINEMATIC REFLEXIVITY

In our dreams we can have our eggs cooked exactly how we want them, but we can't eat them.

> Anna Freud, quoted in Adam Phillips, *On Balance*

Isn't desire always the same, whether the object is present or absent? Isn't the object *always* absent?

> Roland Barthes, *A Lover's Discourse*

When you sleep, you don't control your dream. I like to dive into a dream world that I've made, a world I chose and that I have complete control over.

> David Lynch, in Michael Chion, *David Lynch*

Fantasy is ultimately always the fantasy of a successful sexual relationship.

> Slavoj Žižek, *Tarrying with the Negative: Kant, Hegel and the Critique of Ideology*

D AVID LYNCH'S MULHOLLAND DRIVE has bedazzled and confounded critics and spectators since its release in 2001. It has been characterized as "a mystery that does not want to be solved," "a dead-end journey," and "a head-scratcher" that lacks continuity. Commentators claim that its images "mean nothing in a conventional plot sense" and advise those "requiring logic" to see something else. These reactions seem justified by the movie's intricate narrative pattern, which asks of viewers to "hold multiple understandings in suspense."[1] The film's reflexive nature, its sustained engagement with the economic and ethical crises of Hollywood, has received ample notice. At the time of its release, this was Lynch's most reflexive project, more so than *Lost Highway* (1997), which makes references to home videos and the porn industry. *Mulholland Drive* calls attention to itself as a cinematic construct in a variety of ways: for example, it explores the film-making milieu (it incorporates actors' auditions, backstage scenes, pre-production meetings), exposes the processes of film production (cameras and film apparatus are visible on the screen), foregrounds filmic technique (it has flimsily connected episodes and a non-linear narrative), and flaunts the artifice of film by displaying stylized costumes, hairdo, and make-up from the 1960s. Critics have seen it as a mirror of cinematic genres – the gangster film, the film noir, the western, the musical, the horror film, and the family melodrama – and as a pastiche of Hollywood movies such as *The Wizard of Oz* (1939), Billy Wilder's *Sunset Boulevard* (1950), Alfred Hitchcock's *Vertigo* (1958), and Ingmar Bergman's *Persona* (1966).[2]

In this chapter, I look at the film's reflexivity through the lens of its narrative structure. The latter has proved a complicated issue. In his enigmatic DVD "Synopsis," Lynch provides the headings of a tripartite division of *Mulholland Drive* whose content could be summarized as follows: (1) "She Found Herself the Perfect Mystery": Rita's car crash, the mob subplot, the mystery of Rita's identity, and the discovery of a woman's corpse; (2) "A Sad Illusion": Rita's blond wig, Club Silencio, and the unraveling of Diane's fantasy; (3) "Love": Camilla's betrayal of Diane, Diane's plot to have Camilla murdered, Diane's breakdown and suicide. Critics have typically reduced this schema to a bipartite structure that subsumes parts 1 and 2 into Diane's fantasy and assigns part 3 to her reality from which the fantasy is retroactively constructed. Although this division deploys the pertinent, in my view, contrast between dream/fantasy and waking life/reality, it fails to do justice to the film's narrative complexity and affective power. Therefore, I propose that we conceive of *Mulholland Drive* as a film (Outer Box) that contains four segments (Inner Boxes) arranged on a horizontal plane: a prelude, two narratives, and a coda.[3] These segments are what the viewer sees, four "boxes" of filmic material placed one after another. The prelude (Inner Box 1) depicts a jitterbug contest that Diane once entered and won; the Betty/Rita narrative (Inner Box 2) is Diane's fantasy, which precedes Inner Box 3 on the level of the plot and succeeds it on the level of the story;[4] the Diane/Camilla narrative (Inner Box 3) is Diane's reality, an assemblage of events from her waking life, memories that explain psychologically some of the fantasy's particulars, and brief hallucinatory spells; and the coda (Inner Box 4), a string of disjointed images which, like the prelude, are devoid of dialogue. Although fantasy and reality constitute the ontological realms of Inner Boxes 2 and 3, respectively, as organizing principles of plot and action they are internal to *all* Inner Boxes, weaving like a double thread the film's piebald tapestry.[5]

This quadripartite structure conceives of Diane's life as a narrative that unfolds over time, stitching together her precarious identity out of dreams of Hollywood stardom until it falls apart: Inner Box 1 shows a crucial moment in her past that provides the impetus for a career as an actress; Inner Boxes 2 and 3 constitute her present, her role in *Mulholland Drive* ending with her suicide; and Inner Box 4 is her future or afterlife, what remains of the previous three boxes after the aspiring film star has killed herself. This structure shows more starkly than the dominant bipartite one the essential lack of identity of the main character played by Naomi Watts: in Inner Box 1 a nameless "nobody" wins a dance contest; in Inner Boxes 2 and 3 the winner of the dance contest fractures in many personas of many names; and in Inner Box 4 the dead winner of the dance contest is resurrected as the happy member of an imaginary love union. Prelude and coda thus frame the two narratives and accentuate their play with identity. The quadripartite structure also emphasizes the fact that Diane is always and inescapably the object of the gaze, either Lynch's (Inner Boxes 1, 3, and 4) or her own (Inner Box 2).[6] The centrality of the gaze becomes clearer if we think of Inner Box 2 as a vertically structured container of two boxes, one embedded within the other: Inner Box 2A (Club Silencio) and Inner Box 2B (Blue Box).[7] This vertical configuration of nested Chinese boxes is the spatial dimension along which Diane sees herself and mirrors the film's quadripartite horizontal structure by engaging with its main theme, Diane's precarious identity, from a different perspective: whereas on the horizontal plane Lynch depicts the narrative of Diane's life as an aspiring actress (objective or public viewpoint), on the vertical plane Diane's subconscious fashions a fantasmatic rewriting of this narrative, her personal drama of vision (subjective or private viewpoint).

This architecture allows us to see Mulholland Drive as a multilayered commentary on the relationship between two factors that govern every artistic creation: reality, the economic forces that promote or crush artistic dreams, and fantasy, the artist's attempt to overcome these forces (when they are perceived to be inimical to his or her vision) through defiant acts of the imagination. Since the interplay between these two factors informs film-making – especially, as we shall see, the vexed production of Mulholland Drive – Lynch transmogrifies his experience with this film into the film itself. In so doing, he creates a self-reflexive project that is a dense meditation on film in general and its own production history in particular. Despite the fact that Inner Box 4 (on the horizontal plane) and Inner Box 2B (on the vertical plane) end in a kind of cessation or void – the word "silence" followed by darkness, and darkness, respectively – each box constitutes the last part of a narrative that has already unfolded. This means that Lynch and Diane have managed to direct and film their script – they have had their respective fantasies – and have thus triumphed over the forces of reality opposing them. From this point of view, Mulholland Drive is an ode to cinematic imagination and creativity, its ability to overcome obstacles and produce beautiful works of art.

Born of adversity: the history and the Outer Box of Mulholland Drive

Mulholland Drive is an apt illustration of what philosophers call "creativity under constraint," the transformation of an artistic failure into a success.[8] Lynch's idea for the film was originally pitched to ABC (American Broadcasting Company) as a 1999 television pilot, much like Twin Peaks (1990–91).[9] The pilot follows the first hour of the film and ends with the discovery of a corpse in Diane Selwyn's apartment, Rita cutting her hair short and dyeing it blonde, and the sudden appearance of the Bum at the back of Winkie's.[10] The network liked the script but found the pilot much longer than desired. Lynch sliced off thirty-seven minutes but to no avail. After the French company Studio Canal+ stepped in, he was able to reshoot and edit the television product into a feature film.[11]

This experience, echoing as it did the forced alterations to Dune (1984) and the problems with the last series of Twin Peaks, exasperated Lynch: "At a certain point you realize that you're in with the wrong people. Their thinking process is very foreign to me. They like a fast pace and a linear story, but you want your creations to come out of *you*, and be distinctive. I feel it's possibly true that there are aliens on earth, and they work in television."[12] These "aliens" appeal to popular taste and represent the economic realities governing the production and distribution of films. Their insistence on controlling the artistic process and its outcome may clash with the director's vision. Lynch is acutely aware of this potential conflict: "I always worry about someone forcing me to do things because I identify so much with my work. If certain demands go against what I believe to be correct, it's a horror. And I worry about these things. . . . I think that everybody has had that experience – where you think you've got the situation under control and suddenly you begin to get the feeling that you're a pawn in a much bigger game."[13] Lynch eventually won this "game" by transmuting an apparent failure into a staggering success.

The clash between, on the one hand, an external, threatening, and seemingly omnipotent reality, and, on the other hand, the creative work of unbridled fantasy enters into *Mulholland Drive* and informs its four boxes, both formally and thematically. In Inner Box 1, blurred figures move across a purple screen and are gradually registered as dancers of the jitterbug.[14] As the music hits full swing, more figures appear and merge with one another or are set against empty silhouettes of dancing couples; the effect is that of a collage of colliding images or worlds. The idea of the multiplication of the self is thus introduced. Many of the dancers are twin or triple couples of the same man and woman doing different moves at different spots in the frame, appearing both in the foreground as fully realized entities and in the background as barely discriminable human bodies. A shimmering haze emerges from the bottom and is superimposed on the scene. The haze resolves into the faces of an elderly couple and of a woman later revealed as Diane basking in applause. The focus is unstable, the colors supersaturated. The scene looks like a snapshot of a success story that Diane dreamed up. This impression is strengthened when the camera dissolves to a jerky panning shot that eventually registers as an extreme close-up of the site of dreams, a bed with rose-colored sheets. In Inner Box 3, however, Diane says that she actually won a jitterbug contest that "sort of led to acting, to wanting to act." Interestingly, Diane is not shown among the contestants; her victory is severed from her dance performance and can be inferred only from her triumphant expression. The dissociation of her performance from its outcome foreshadows an idea that receives prominence in Inner Box 2, namely that success in Hollywood may have little or nothing to do with actual talent. Actors get roles not necessarily because they are good – in Inner Boxes 2 and 3 Camilla Rhodes is the appointed winner of the parts that Betty never competes for and Diane oddly loses – but because they have influential agents who promote them.

Although Inner Box 2 is Diane's fantasy, it has the texture of reality by observing the spatio-temporal logic, coherence, and linear progression of events normally associated with narrative renditions of waking life. By contrast, the editing of Inner Box 3 induces spatial and temporal disorientation: persons and events are desultory, flashbacks and hallucinations abound. In addition, Inner Boxes 2 and 3 are equally unreliable from an epistemological point of view: qua fantasy Inner Box 2 is a piece of fiction, while Inner Box 3 depicts the reality of a delusional woman on the verge of suicide whose memories cannot be trusted.[15] The interweaving of fantasy and reality is also a thematic concern of the film, and below I discuss its deployment in Inner Box 2 (see sections below, "Diane's Fantasy," "Diane's Fantasy Onstage," and "Diane's Fantasy Dissolved"). For the moment and in anticipation of that discussion, I note one of its most prominent applications, the characters' identity shifts between Inner Boxes 2 and 3. These shifts involve not only nominal changes – e.g. Coco Lenoix (Ann Miller) in Inner Box 2 becomes Coco Kesher in Inner Box 3 – but also physical and psychological mutations, such as Diane's bifurcation into Betty and Camilla (the latter being the Rita of Inner Box 3): in Inner Box 2, Betty looks like Diane but her actions evince Camilla's self-assertiveness, whereas at first Rita is Camilla's physical and Diane's psychological doppelgänger but later she looks like Diane and manifests some of Camilla's independence.

Finally, Inner Box 4 consists of three scenes of a symbolic valence. The first scene is a smoky close-up of a Bum (Bonnie Aarons) who lurks behind Winkie's restaurant, a cross between a man and an animal. A personification of evil rather than a readily identifiable entity, the Bum lies outside Diane's consciousness whose death he survives, just as Bob is independent of Laura Palmer in *Fire Walk with Me* (1992). The second scene is a series of blue-tinted, overexposed head shots of Betty/Diane and Rita/Camilla: the two women look like copies of invented originals, lovers relishing a union that they had neither in Inner Box 2 nor in Inner Box 3. The third scene shows the empty stage of club Silencio with the blue-haired Lady (Cori Glazer) sitting above it and whispering "Silencio."

Her presence is clearly extradiegetic, and her utterance marks an end, perhaps that of Diane's life, or of Mulholland Drive, or of film in general.[16] She may even represent television producers shutting down pilots, or the Hollywood industry terminating film careers. Yet silence need not be final but only an interstice, the gap between two sounds, just as silence in music can be a pause before the resumption of sound. From this point of view, this mysterious figure could stand for Lynch requesting silence to create another film (in which case "silencio" would be equivalent to a director's final "cut"). Her appearance in an empty space at the end of the movie contrasts with the noisy jitterbug contest at the beginning and underlies the futility of Diane's quest for professional success – there is no applause for Diane, just silence.

Diane's fantasy: Inner Box 2

With a running time of approximately two hours, Inner Box 2 is as long as the average feature film and can fruitfully be seen as a film within a film. In it Diane plays a double role: at the extradiegetic level, registered spatially as the bed with the rose-colored sheets, she is Lynch's proxy, the director who dreams up a fantasy of personal and professional success in a state of utter freedom from external constraints; at the diegetic level, marked by the immersion of the camera into the pillow (a metonymy for Diane's head), she bifurcates into (at least) two female personas, to each of whom she imparts her physical and/or mental attributes: the perky blonde Betty Elms (Naomi Watts), an ambitious and talented actress, and the amnesiac brunette Rita (Laura Elena Harring) with whom Betty falls in love. Although critics tend to identify Betty with Diane and Rita with Camilla, I see Diane primarily as a hybrid of Betty and Rita, and secondarily as a "composite structure" of all the female leads in her fantasy (which includes the blonde Camilla Rhodes).[17] In addition, Diane invents the figure of the unsuccessful director, Adam Kesher (Justin Theroux), who acts as her foil qua director of Inner Box 2 (and as Lynch's foil qua director of Mulholland Drive). Inner Box 2 is Diane's artistic feat, which mirrors Lynch's cinematic accomplishment in its deployment of the trope of the good/successful versus the bad/unsuccessful director and actor: the successful and uncompromising director (Lynch of the feature film, Diane) pulls off his/her dream project, whereas the director who willy-nilly capitulates to the system merely attempts to pull off his project (Lynch of the pilot, Adam Kesher of *The Sylvia North Story*);[18] the good actress, Betty, shines at the rehearsal, and her physical lookalike, Camilla Rhodes (Melissa George), gets the role at the audition (both are stand-ins for Diane), whereas the brunette singer who auditions for Adam Kesher (a stand-in for Camilla of Inner Box 3) loses to the blonde Camilla/Diane.[19]

That Diane can be seen as an extension of Lynch qua director of her fantasy is a plausible assumption given the similarities between film and dream. The phenomenology of a film is similar to that of a dream: the spectator watches the film, just as the dreamer sees his or her dream. An analogy of being obtains between film and dream: they both *are* in the same way. In addition, film spectator and dreamer inhabit a different space and time from the immaterial characters in the film and the dream, respectively. The fact that film is projected alters its tense – it must necessarily *have been* photographed and processed in the past – and dreams are imaginative re-creations of past events. Psychoanalysis thinks of dreams as projected on a screen: "the dream screen, blank surface present in dreams though mostly unseen is covered over by the manifest content of the projected dream."[20] Yet the film's time, as well as the dream's time, is largely indeterminate: "The [cinematic] image is the imprint of a particular moment whose particularity becomes indeterminable precisely because the image does not speak its own relation to time. Film *is*, therefore, a record of time, but a nonspecific, nonidentifiable time, a disembodied, unanchored time."[21] The images on the screen, the darkness of the movie theater, the immobility of the spectator, simulate the atmosphere of a dream.[22] Finally, Diane's fantasy "comes out of her," and Lynch's films, ideally, "come out of him" without the intervention of external forces.

The central theme of Diane's fantasy is the quest for Rita's identity. The mystery or detective story is ideally suited to this project because of its epistemophilic drive, the desire to uncover hidden truths and the deferral of its gratification. As in the traditional narrative of resolution, so in *Mulholland Drive* there is a sense of problem solving, of things being worked out in some way. Roland Barthes uses the term "hermeneutic" to describe this function, which "articulate[s] in various ways a question, its response and the variety of chance events which can either formulate the question or delay its answer."[23] Lynch describes his approach to scriptwriting in a way that evokes the writing of a detective story: "Ideas never really come all at once for a whole feature anyway. They come in fragments. So you could stop at any moment and say: 'These are my fragments: how will I ever get to a whole movie from these?' But those fragments are compelling other fragments to join them. With *Mulholland Drive* I had a whole bunch of a certain type of fragments – open-ended fragments. So they needed a certain type of idea to come and tie them together. That was the trick."[24] Just as the clues of a mystery point to a solution that makes them intelligible qua clues, so fragments of a whole become meaningful once they have been embedded into the system in which they belong. A successful mystery story, as well as a Lynch film, is like a puzzle that proceeds to its (dis)solution under the author's (and director's) firm control. For Lynch, the search for the answer must be suspenseful: "It's so beautiful not knowing where [the movie] is going at first, and to discover it through action and reaction.[25] It would be great if you could work like that all the time. I don't blame people for wanting to know what's going to happen next – they're bankrolling it, and it's a huge expense. But it would be no fun if you knew everything upfront. It would just be a job."[26] Lynch demands control in the editing room, where he pieces together his film mystery, but during filming he welcomes accidents, which boost creativity.

Inner Box 2 is also the product of authorial control and accident. Diane dreams up her story and assigns roles to her actors. In Betty she creates an idealized persona of herself and puts her in charge of the quest for Rita's identity, a woman whose dependence on the strong and assertive Betty echoes Diane's dependence on Camilla. Betty initiates the investigation into Rita's past, masterminds the moves, and provides emotional support, while Rita is passive and aimless, like the emotionally weary and professionally stranded Diane. Betty is Diane's physical twin, and Rita is her psychological twin. These two parts of Diane's personality occasionally converge. When Coco, for example, drops by to see Betty, she spots Rita sitting on the couch and asks, "Who are you?" The amnesiac Rita cannot think of an answer and stumbles, "Uh, Betty?" By calling for her friend, Rita calls herself Betty and thus unwittingly identifies herself as Betty.[27] Although Diane's fantasy creates a world in which Betty gets what Diane craves, elements from her reality creep into the fantasy. Think of Louise Bonner (Lee Grant), the spooky psychic who shows up at Aunt Ruth's apartment and says that something is "terribly wrong." When Ruth's niece tells Louise that her name is Betty, the psychic shakes her head and moans, "No it's not." Here Diane's reality enters her fantasy and casts doubt upon Betty's fictional identity. Or think of the decomposing corpse of a woman (Lyssie Powell) that Betty and Rita discover in Diane's apartment in Sierra Bonita. Here Diane's fantasy fuses two time slices and two corpses: the corpse is a hybrid of the already dead Camilla (the Rita of Inner Box 3) and the soon-to-commit-suicide Diane; it is both a signifier of a past event and a premonition of a future occurrence.[28]

Adam Kesher represents the frustrated Lynch of the television pilot and serves as Diane's foil qua director of her fantasy. Professionally, he struggles against the machinations of Mr Roque, a man bound to a wheelchair and placed in a vault of glass and red velvet, a Hollywood tycoon who wields ultimate power with a chilling detachment and resolve: he shuts down Adam's production and freezes his bank accounts.[29] His emissaries, the Castigliane brothers (Dan Hedaya and Angelo Badalamenti), invade the pre-production meeting and dictate the choice of the female lead by proffering Camilla Rhodes' head shot and repeating the words, "This is the girl." When Adam protests, "There is no way that girl is in my movie; that girl is not in my film," one of the brothers informs him in a manner that brooks no disagreement, "It's no longer your film." Another of Mr Roque's associates, the Cowboy (Monty Montgomery), specifies the condition under which Adam can remain the director, namely that Camilla Rhodes be the lead.

Adam reacts vindictively and ineffectually. He attacks the limousine of the Castigliane brothers with a golf club (an obvious phallic symbol) and pours pink paint into his wife's jewelry box after he catches her in bed with the pool man (her adultery puts the lie to his showy manliness). The lover intervenes in the ensuing fight between husband and wife and kicks Adam out of the house. With his clothes covered in pink paint and a bloody nose Adam lodges in a seedy hotel downtown where he finds out that he is broke.[30] His rage soon gives way to resignation: his words at the audition are those of the Castigliane brothers and the Cowboy, the code of his submission: "This is the girl." Adam has been viewed as "a stand-in for Lynch, who is known to fear creative interference of any sort."[31] More precisely, however, he represents the Lynch of the television pilot who was forced to entertain various compromises, one of which involved the choice of the lead actresses.[32]

Diane also casts Betty as one of the leads of Inner Box 2. Given the space constraints, I shall look briefly at two scenes in which Betty, a character of Diane's script, redoubles her fictiveness by "pretend[ing] to be someone else," a nameless character in a script-within-the-script. The first scene is a dry run of her part played with Rita, and the second scene is the audition of that part at the studio.[33] Let me first say a few words about the scene. Betty plays a young woman who thwarts the erotic advances of her father's friend played by the experienced actor Woody Katz (Chad Everett). The scenario is trite – Betty calls it "lame" – but the scene is psychologically complex, as Betty must resist a man for whom she feels a powerful and illicit attraction. Her frustrated passion for the forbidden/unattainable object of desire mirrors Diane's relationship with Camilla, and several of Betty's lines are covert allusions to Diane's crime. For example, the line, "You are playing a dangerous game here that is not going to work," is a threat aimed implicitly at Diane as the mastermind of the plan to have Camilla killed. Diane's self-hatred and hatred of Camilla are reflected in the line, "I hate you, I hate us both." Her wrongdoing is alluded to in the threat, "I will kill you," while her fear of being arrested is conveyed by her partner's utterance, "Then they will put you in jail."[34] The script is a fantasy-within-the-fantasy, an opportunity for Diane to do what she fails to do in her waking life, namely resist her passion for Camilla and entertain murder as a mere possibility.

At the dry run, Rita impersonates Betty's co-star and woodenly cues his lines. Betty bristles with anger and brandishes a dinner knife in front of Rita. At the end of the scene, the latter exclaims, "You're really good!" Here Rita assumes the double role of cooperative lover and adulatory audience, thereby offering Betty/Diane the validation that she craves. At the audition, Betty is once again good but completely different. Her performance is subtle and nuanced. Simulating Camilla's dominance in Diane's life, Woody looks smug and in control of the situation, but soon Betty counters his brusque sexuality and starts directing the scene.[35] When Woody's hand touches the rear of Betty's skirt, Betty's hand presses it against herself harder than her co-star dared to. By the end of the scene, sexual aggression is laden with a vague sense of menace, as Betty places an arm with a closed fist around Woody's neck and initiates a long, open-mouth kiss. Her clenched fist evokes the knife that she held earlier in front of Rita, only this time the weapon is her lethal sexual power.

Betty's transformation from an angry woman in the dry run to a sultry seductress in the audition is striking. Phillip Lopate sees it as "the playful fluidity that represents, for Lynch, the promise of human character, the reverse side of the anxiety that comes of not having a fixed self." Performance celebrates the instability of identity; in Lopate's words, "where identity is not fixed, performance becomes a floating anchor."[36] But in this particular enactment of the fluidity of identity we can also detect echoes of Diane's relationship with Camilla. The murderous Betty of the dry run is the vindictive Diane who has hired a hit man to kill her lover, whereas the sexually confident Betty of the audition is the twin of the Camilla of Inner Box 3. In the former scene, Betty enacts the frustrated Diane (dry runs are, after all, not the real thing), and in the latter scene, where good performance is of the essence, she plays the self-assured Camilla. By letting Betty take on Camilla's personality, Diane symbolically kills her lover: if Betty can assimilate Camilla, the latter is expendable. Betty's acting wins her the approval of two different audiences: Rita congratulates her enactment of Diane's personality, and the assembled audience at the studio applauds her performance of Camilla's personality. Betty succeeds where Diane fails because she represents the best of both worlds: she has Diane's actorly skill and Camilla's sexual allure. As the quintessential performer Betty can become anything she wants because she is nothing in particular.

Diane's fantasy onstage: Club Silencio or Inner Box 2A

Club Silencio is a pivotal scene of the film. After their love-making, Betty and Rita fall asleep. The camera registers their consummation as a becalmed and satisfied union: their hands are intertwined, their faces are completing one another, or better, unfolding into one another, a shot evocative of Picasso's *Dora Maar*. In the early hours of the morning, Rita rouses her mate with outbursts of the Spanish words "Silencio," "No hay banda," and "No hay orquesta," and takes her to the club Silencio, a half-empty cabaret reminiscent of *Twin Peaks'* Red Room. Its stage is lined with red walls and velvety curtains that recall Mr Roque's room, and a gleaming chrome microphone is placed mid-stage. Betty and Rita enter and sit among the audience. This is the only time that Rita dons her blonde wig in public, and her physical resemblance to Betty is striking.

The shooting of the scene in a theatrical space calls attention to the illusory nature of performance. Film conflates actor with character, and the cinematic world is perceived as reality; in Leo Braudy's words, "Film acting is less impersonation than personation, part of personality but not identifiable with it."[37] By contrast, the three-dimensionality of the stage makes it harder for the theater to convince the audience of the verisimilitude of its events; the spectator is constantly aware of the actor's impersonation. In addition, editing splices together cinematic time and space and thus eliminates the fissures that in the theater would result from changes of lighting and sets.[38] The viewer's sympathetic identification with the stage actor must constantly wrestle with his/her awareness of the artificiality of the spectacle. Furthermore, the stage invites the viewers' gaze because the theater is predicated on the reciprocal awareness of the presence of actors and spectators, whereas the cinematic action is "unaware of our existence and is part of the universe."[39] In Club Silencio, Betty and Rita become spectators of a performance staged by Diane qua director of Inner Box 2, and thus they represent the film's extradiegetic viewers. Unlike Betty and Rita, however, the film's spectators watch the events onstage through two frames, that of the screen and that of the proscenium, a double perspective that compounds the artifice and parallels Diane's double perspective of the same events, that of the eye of her "camera" and that of the proscenium. Finally, the theater is bound up with mortality (an important theme of the film), since the theatrical event is born and dies every night. This is not the case with film, where repeated viewings of the same movie create the impression of an ever-renewed present.

Club Silencio calls attention to performance as sleight-of-hand. Like Mann's Cipolla, the stage magician (Richard Green) waves his hands in the direction of an unseen band, summons the sound of music, and by breaking "the fourth wall" tells the audience in English, French, and Spanish that "there is no band." After tossing aside his cane, which makes no sound as it exits the film frame, he calls for a trumpet player, one appears and seems to play his trumpet, but when he removes it from his mouth, the sound continues; he is merely mimicking a recorded trumpet. We hear a clarinet and a trombone, yet there are no musicians on sight; the music is taped. What ought to be a live performance is transformed into a mechanical reproduction of a past live experience. The best example of this dissociation of the aural from the visual is Rebekah Del

Rio's rendition of a Spanish version of Roy Orbison's song "Crying."[40] When the singer collapses, her body is carried offstage, while her voice continues to intone. The entire time she has been lip-syncing a song recorded from her own voice, just as the female singers auditioning for Adam Kesher do not engage in live performance but lip-sync oldies.[41] Her lip-syncing stands for the borrowed "voices," the illusions and fantasies that the film industry distributes to those wishing to inhabit "the dream place" called Hollywood. Her expressionless and motionless body turns her into a human "tape recorder" onstage. Because anyone can lip-sync a recorded song, Del Rio's physical presence becomes utterly dispensable, a mere stage prop that symbolizes "the disposable woman whose energy briefly attracts and enchants."[42]

Club Silencio stresses cinematic reflexivity by enacting the experience of making and watching films: it foregrounds performance, displays the agencies involved in it, and calls attention to the core filmic relationship between sight and sound.[43] It also encompasses elements of the entire film: the mysterious blue-haired Lady in the balcony above the stage possibly represents the omnipotent Hollywood producers; the musicians and the singer stand for the film's actors and the characters populating Diane's fantasy; and the stage magician functions as a stand-in for the illusionists Lynch, Diane, and Adam Kesher.[44] A muffled explosion recalls the sound at the end of the jitterbug contest in Inner Box 1, and the thick smoke into which the stage magician disappears recalls the smoke coming out of Rita's car crash and anticipates the smoke around Diane's bed after she has committed suicide. Del Rio's song of a lost love object alludes to Diane's unrequited love for Camilla.[45] The singer's split into the Deleuzian "opsign" (her body collapses) and "sonsign" (her recorded voice continues to sing) illustrates the disjunction between a present and a past event. Because sounds come from somewhere, our hearing them calls attention to an invisible source and conveys the impossibility of assimilating Diane's past guilt into her present fantasy. Adam Kesher's utterance, "This is the girl," is another example of a character's making sounds that originate outside himself – the Castigliane brothers/the Cowboy in Inner Box 2, and Diane in Inner Box 3 (this is the way in which Diane transfers to the mob and the Cowboy her guilt for Camilla's murder; these are the cold executioners of an implacable will).[46] The severance of the visual from the aural suggests that Del Rio is and is not who she is, in the sense that she is physically the singer by that name but she is not currently singing the song we hear. Similarly, Betty and Rita are and are not who they are, in the sense that they are the visible characters of Diane's dream but they are also the fictive products of the subconscious of a film character who is herself the flickering image of an actress projected through celluloid. This ontological ambivalence foregrounds mechanical reproduction, the very technique of film production, and underscores the fact that Del Rio, Betty, Rita, and Diane are *all* film performers. Del Rio's first name (Rebekah) is a sort of hybrid of Rita and Betty, while her red and black dress combines the colors of their clothes. Her collapse echoes Rita's collapse upon coming out of the car wreckage and qua simulation of dying it echoes Camilla's death and foreshadows Diane's suicide. Del Rio is yet another cipher, the double of Betty-cum-Rita (and of Diane) now (dis)placed on stage. This underlies the reflexive nature of Diane's gaze: the dreamer simultaneously watches and is being watched, as in a mirror. Club Silencio thus becomes Diane's private theater, the playground of her obsessions and delusions.

Club Silencio dramatizes the spectator's seduction by the performance. Although Betty and Rita are repeatedly told of the illusory nature of the stage events, they collude in their own deception. Enacting the song's lyrics, they lovingly hold one another and weep; like another Diane, Del Rio manipulates their reactions. Rita comforts Betty who convulses violently – a visual sign of internal transformation that links *Mulholland Drive* with *Lost Highway* and an analogue of the "movement" created by cinematic editing. Their emotional connection, captured by exquisite close-ups, illustrates Diane's affective integration: the formerly divided Diane between a brave Betty and a fearful Rita is now unified. The scene thus achieves the opposite of Brecht's *Verfremdungseffekt* or "alienation effect": whereas his plays flag the artifice of performance in order to induce in the viewer an awareness of the theatrical illusion, the magician implicates the spectators in the system by exposing the theatrical pretense. In Inner Box 2, Betty and Rita are in the spotlight and unselfconsciously perform Diane's fantasy, but in Inner Box 2A, they – and a fortiori Diane – sit beyond the footlights and must confront the illusory nature of the fantasy, "the pure, contentless impossible object."[47] The two women look at Del Rio the way fans look at stage actors, so that the illusion of the stage signifies the illusion of stardom. Diane's fantasy makes prominent the mechanism and agents of film-making and thus contains the seeds of its own dissolution. The Hollywood industry has penetrated even her subconscious and undermines her redemptive story from within. This is the moment of the returned gaze, of the *voyeuse vue*, which ruptures the illusion.[48] At this point, Diane has taken on every role available to her – director, actor, and spectator – and must soon yield to the cumulative weight of her fantasmatic omnipotence. Consciousness is coming back, and she is about to awaken and face her grim reality; to paraphrase Rita, "the sleep did not do it."

Diane's fantasy dissolved: Blue Box or Inner Box 2B

While Del Rio's body is being carried off stage, Betty opens her purse and finds in it a blue box. She and Rita return hastily to the apartment and soon disappear from frame and film. Betty exits right away, while Rita vanishes after she has opened the blue box with the blue key, which Betty stashed away in a blue hatbox in the bedroom closet. The blue box is shown to be empty, and Lynch's camera is subsumed by its dark interior. Within seconds the box drops to the floor, and the owner of the apartment (Aunt Ruth in Inner Box 3) walks in. The camera shifts to a sleeping Diane in her bedroom, a visual segue to the realm of reality or Inner Box 3.

Placed as it is in two enclosures, one within the other – Betty's purse and Club Silencio – the blue box is the material representation of the Chinese box structure of Inner Box 2. Betty's purse alludes to the economic powers that make possible the production of films. Inner Box 2B thus echoes Lynch's experience with the television pilot and Adam Kesher's dealings with Mr Roque and his ilk. It is also a visual reminder of Rita's purse, itself the fantasy equivalent of Diane's purse, which contains the money for Camilla's murder. The blue box brings to mind Club Silencio: its color evokes the club's dominant color, and its shape recalls that of the stage with the raised lid representing the rear wall of the stage. When the box is closed, it is pregnant with possibilities and induces hope; it is hardly an accident that Inner Box 2 unfolds while the blue box remains unlocked. Once open, however, it is shown to be empty, and the fantasy ends. Just as Club Silencio turns Betty and Rita into spectators of a declared illusion, so the empty blue box confronts Diane with the illusoriness of her fantasy.

Critics have seen the blue box as "the darkness that has been waiting since the beginning of the film," as "Pandora's box . . . that symbolizes the knowledge that Diane ordered Camilla's murder," or as a representation of the "void that exists between fantasy and desire."[49] Psychoanalytically, the conjunction of box and key, the moment of unlocking, signifies "the intersection of fantasy and reality. The blue key is the literal key to Diane's repressed truth, her reality principle, so that, once used, it destroys the possibility of her escape from guilt."[50] Clearly, the blue key is the fantasy equivalent of the blue key that the hit man agreed to leave with Diane as proof that Camilla was dead. The key to the box is found in Rita's purse at the beginning of Inner Box 2 because it represents the execution of Camilla's murder, which has already taken place. By contrast, the empty blue box appears at the end of Inner Box 2 because its presence marks the end of the fantasy.[51] The unlocking of Betty's box by Rita's key signifies the moment at which the inescapable factuality of Camilla's murder (key) penetrates the fantasy (box) whose purpose was to block the murder from view. Fantasy cannot appease guilt, only death can. From a broader perspective, the unlocked blue box reveals the illusory nature of film as such, the fact that it *is* nothing other than what it *shows*: as the camera is sucked into the box, its lens becomes coextensive with the box's empty space and, like Alice falling through the rabbit hole in one of Lynch's favorite movies, the spectator's gaze falls through the box.

Where does all this leave us? "Silencio" is the declaration, the request, or the command at the end of the film, the enigmatic utterance that seems to connote resignation, impatience, irritation, and a sense of finality, all at once. Susan Sontag views silence as "the artist's ultimate other-worldly gesture: by silence, he frees himself from servile bondage to the world, which appears as patron, client, consumer, antagonist, arbiter, and distorter of his work."[52] *Mulholland Drive* is an elegiac testimony to the artist's ability to liberate himself/herself from servility to the Hollywood industry by exposing, overcoming, and eventually transcending that servility in death, both *in* the film and *of* the film. But it is also a work that celebrates love, its fleeting pleasures, vagaries, deceptions, and woes, captivating and enchanting its viewers.[53]

Notes

1 These quotations come from David Andrews, "An Oneiric Fugue: The Various Logics of Mulholland Drive," Journal of Film and Video 56 (2004): 25–40.

2 For a brief discussion of some of the film's reflexive elements see Robert Sinnerbrink's essay in this volume.

3 Andrews, "Oneiric Fugue,"deploys the idiom of "boxes" but puts it to a different use.

4 Plot is the ordered structure of what is visually or linguistically narrated: it is what we see on screen, images composed in a certain sequential order. Story, on the other hand, is the narration of events in chronological order, which viewers understand by reconstructing an account of events from the visual and narrative cues composing the plot. For the use of the Russian formalist distinction between plot (syuzhet) and story (fabula) in film see David Bordwell, Narration in the Fiction Film (Madison: University of Wisconsin Press, 1985), pp. 49–53.

5 The painting by Guido Reni, Beatrice Cenci, which hangs on the hallway of Aunt Ruth's apartment, is a framed or "boxed" visual evocation of a story that has elements of Diane's tragedy. The picture is a miniature representation of the moving picture and another reflexive element since its inclusion calls attention to the screen as a two-dimensional surface. We see the illuminated figure of Beatrice Cenci, a young Italian noblewoman who fell victim to her father's incestuous advances. Beatrice, her siblings, and stepmother hired two vassals who helped them to drug the father, and then the family bludgeoned him to death with a hammer and threw the body off the balcony to make it look like an accident. With the exception of the youngest son, the killers were apprehended and executed; Beatrice was beheaded. The painting is like a frozen frame that memorializes Beatrice, turning her into the stuff of legend much like the shot of a luminous Diane (minus the elderly couple) in Inner Box 1 or that of her in Inner Box 4 (minus Rita/Camilla). I am grateful to C. D. C. Reeve for calling my attention to the painting and causing me to think about its contribution to the film.

6 Of course Lynch is still looking at Diane in Inner Box 2, but what matters is that Diane is looking at herself.

7 The terms "Club Silencio" and "Blue Box" refer to the relevant scenes, whereas the terms "club Silencio" and "blue box" refer to the relevant place and object in the film.

8 See Mjette Hort (ed.), Dekalog 1: On the Five Obstructions (London: Wallflower, 2008). Lynch echoes the idea of "creativity under constraint" in Catching the Big Fish: Meditation, Consciousness, and Creativity (London: Bobkind 2006), pp. 111–12.

9 For the production history of Mulholland Drive see, for example, Tad Friend, "Creative Differences," New Yorker, 6 September 1999, pp. 56–67, and Chris Rodley, Lynch on Lynch (New York: Faber & Faber, 2005), pp. 279–87. For a

comparison of the pilot with the movie see Warren Buckland, "'A Sad, Bad Traffic Accident': The Televisual Prehistory of David Lynch's Film *Mulholland Dr.*," *New Review of Film and Television Studies* 1 (2003): 131–47.

10   For the pilot screenplay of the film see "Mulholland Drive Pilot – The Screenplay," <http://www.lynchnet.com/mdrive/mdscript.html>.

11   For the transformation of the pilot into the feature film see "Mulholland Dr.," featured video, *Club Silencio*, <http://www.mulholland-drive.net>.

12   Friend, "Creative Differences," p. 67 (emphasis original).

13   Rodley, *Lynch on Lynch*, pp. 274–75.

14   Purple combines red and blue, the dominant colors of Inner Boxes 2 and 3.

15   Cf. Andrews, "Oneiric Fugue," p. 30.

16   This last possibility suggests itself in light of Mary Ann Doane's claim that ". . . it is doubtful that any image (in the sound film) is uninflected by sound. This is crucially so, given the fact that in the dominant narrative cinema, sound extends from beginning to the end of the film – sound is never absent (silence is, at the least, room tone). In fact, the lack of any sound is taboo in the editing of the sound track." See "The Voice in the Cinema: The Articulation of Body and Space," in Philip Rosen (ed.), *Narrative, Apparatus, Ideology: A Film Theory Reader* (New York: Columbia University Press, 1986), pp. 335–48.

17   From a Freudian perspective, Diane is herself a dream character, a "composite structure," an entity made out of Hollywood dreams. See Sigmund Freud, *On Dreams*, in *The Freud Reader*, ed. Peter Gay (New York: W. W. Norton & Co., 1995), p. 4.

18   In Inner Box 3, *The Sylvia North Story* receives mention as a finished project with Camilla Rhodes as the lead actress and Bob Brooker as the director (in Inner Box 2 Bob is the director of the doomed film project for which Betty auditions). By contrast, in Inner Box 2 Adam Kesher is shown only at the stages of pre-production and auditioning.

19   Diane's identification with the blonde Camilla Rhodes of Inner Box 2 receives support in Inner Box 3: at Adam's engagement party to Camilla, the blonde Camilla Rhodes kisses the brunette one and glances at Diane with Camilla's red lipstick smeared over her pink lips (the pink is still visible). In this scene, Diane is wearing red lipstick as well, but in Inner Box 2 Betty wears pink lipstick.

20   See Stephen Heath, "Narrative Space," in Philip Rosen (ed.), *Narrative, Apparatus, Ideology: A Film Theory Reader* (New York: Columbia University Press, 1986), pp. 379–420.

21   Mary Ann Doane, *The Emergence of Cinematic Time: Modernity, Contingency, the Archive* (Cambridge, MA: Harvard University Press, 2002), pp. 162–63. In the scene at Winkie's, Dan finds it hard to specify when he saw the dream that he narrates to his friend (or perhaps therapist): "It's not day or night. It's kind of half-night, you know?"

22 See Robert Stam, *Reflexivity in Film and Literature: From Don Quixote to Jean-Luc Godard* (New York: Columbia University Press, 1992), p. 12.

23 Roland Barthes, *S/Z* (New York: Hill & Wang, 1975), p. 17.

24 Rodley, *Lynch on Lynch*, p. 284.

25 At Betty's audition in Inner Box 2, Woody tells the director, "Acting is reacting." The film itself is a complicated series of actions and reactions.

26 Rodley, *Lynch on Lynch*, p. 277.

27 At the same time the question mark at the end of her answer betrays the uncertainty of the answer.

28 The corpse wears a black dress that resembles the dress that Rita wears in the limousine prior to the accident, and her head is battered, as Diane's will be after the gunshot.

29 Michael J. Anderson, who plays Mr Roque, also appears in *Twin Peaks* as the famous backwards-talking "Man from Another Place." Note the irony of casting a dwarf in the role of a studio magnate and that of a man in a wheelchair posing as a free and omnipotent agent.

30 The name "Kesher" evokes "cash" and suggests Adam's capitulation to the economic powers of Hollywood. The name "Adam" alludes to the First Man and his responsibility for humanity's fall from grace – an echo of Diane's fall from a coveted stardom. The pink paint on his clothes associates him visually with Betty who also wears pink clothes, the washed out hue of Camilla's red.

31 Friend, "Creative Differences," p. 61.

32 See Friend, "Creative Differences," pp. 62–63, for this demand placed on Lynch. The network also requested the deletion of certain scenes and objected to some linguistic usage.

33 For a detailed examination of these two scenes see George Toles, "Auditioning Betty in *Mulholland Drive*," *Film Quarterly* 58 (2004): 2–13.

34 After Betty's audition for a movie that was not to be made, Lynnie James, the casting agent, takes her to a studio where Adam Kesher "has a project you will kill," *The Sylvia North Story*. Note the absence of an object – kill what or whom? The future tense points to Diane's suicide, while the act of killing alludes also to Camilla's murder.

35 Woody's reference to the brunette who has already auditioned for Betty's role evokes Camilla and suggests that Betty comes after her.

36 See Lopate, "Welcome to LA: Hollywood Outsider David Lynch Plunges into Tinseltown's Dark Psyche," *Film Comment*, September/October 2001, p. 47.

37 Leo Braudy, "Acting: Stage vs Screen," in Leo Braudy and Marshall Cohen (eds), *Film Theory and Criticism* (Oxford: Oxford University Press, 2004), pp. 429–35.

38 Cf. Debra Shostak, "Dancing in Hollywood's 'Blue Box': Genre and Screen Memories in 'Mulholland Drive,'" *Post Script* 28 (2008), p. 11.

39 André Bazin, "Theater and Cinema – Part Two," in *What Is Cinema?* (Berkeley: University of California Press), p. 102.

40 This is the second time that a character lip-syncs a Roy Orbison song in a Lynch film, the first time being Dean Stockwell's rendition of "In Dreams" in *Blue Velvet*.

41 More similarities can be traced between the auditioning for *The Sylvia North Story* and Club Silencio. As the female performers sing "Sixteen Reasons (Why I Love You)," the camera zooms out – the performers are singing in a box (sound booth); the camera zooms still out – they are singing in a box within a box (the sound stage). The performers, the sound booth, and the stage all signify something other than what they are: the performers are actresses who act as actresses, the sound booth is a non-operational set piece presented as a non-operational set piece for a Hollywood movie, and the sound stage is a set piece for *Mulholland Drive*.

42 Martha P. Nochimson, "'All I Need Is the Girl': The Life and Death of Creativity in *Mulholland Drive*," in Erica Sheen and Annette Davison (eds), *The Cinema of David Lynch: American Dreams, Nightmare Visions* (London: Wallflower Press, 2004), p. 166.

43 The first instance of the dissociation between sight and sound occurs during the transition from Inner Box 1 to Inner Box 2: as the hand-held camera zooms into a rose-colored pillow, we see no sleeping person, yet we hear human breathing.

44 A visual cue uniting the stage magician with Diane is their disappearance in smoke. The use of the same actor (Geno Silva) in the roles of "Cookie," the manager of the dilapidated hotel downtown, and of the stage magician's attendant suggests a connection between the emcee and Adam Kesher.

45 The name given to Del Rio, "La Llorona" ("The Weeping Woman"), is the title of a Hispanic folk tale about a legendary woman who drowns her two children after her husband has left her. She cries every night until she drowns herself, and her crying can be heard at night.

46 A third example of the dissociation of sound and body would be Rita intoning the stage magician's phrases "No hay banda" and "No hay orquesta" when she awakens next to Betty. Although these phrases are heard in the film after Betty and Rita have gone to club Silencio, the stage magician has preceded Rita in uttering them because the show must have taken place before Rita and Diane visited the club. The sound emanates from a machine (tape recorder), an echo of Mr Roque's mechanical voice.

47 Todd McGowan, *The Impossible David Lynch* (New York: Columbia University Press, 2007), pp. 194–219.

48 The people on the stage of club Silencio look at Betty, Rita, and Diane qua director of the scene, thereby implicating them in what is going on. By contrast, in a film the actors normally look away from the camera and thus exclude the viewer from the spectacle.

49 These three quotations come from Martha P. Nochimson, "Review: *Mulholland Drive*," *Film Quarterly* 56 (2002), p. 43; K.N. Hayles and N. Gessler, "The Slipstream of Mixed Reality: Unstable Ontologies and Semiotic Markers in

The Thirteenth Floor, Dark City, and *Mulholland Drive,"* PMLA 119(3) (2004), p. 497; and Todd McGowan, "Lost on *Mulholland Drive:* Navigating David Lynch's Panegyric to Hollywood," *Cinema Journal* 43(2) (2004), p. 83.

50 Shostak, "Dancing in Hollywood's 'Blue Box,'" p. 12.

51 The Cowboy opens the door to Diane's bedroom and says, "Hey, pretty girl, time to wake up." He is the one to end her fantasy because as someone who works with or for Mr Roque he represents the economic powers that control artistic dreams (the Cowboy promotes the project of the compliant Adam Kesher but terminates the dream of Diane's unruly subconscious). As the unwelcome and omnipotent intruder into her dream world, he opens the door to the site of her dreams without knocking, whereas seconds later Diane's uninvited neighbor knocks on the apartment's front door repeatedly and loudly before being admitted inside. The neighbor comes to collect her belongings from Diane's place and thus officially to end their cohabitation (and perhaps love affair). Her arrival at the beginning of Inner Box 3 marks an end and mirrors the Cowboy's termination of Diane's fantasy at the end of Inner Box 2. The transition from the dream world to the real world is characterized by loss that reflects Diane's double loss of a career in Hollywood and Camilla's love.

52 Susan Sontag, "The Aesthetics of Silence," in *Styles of Radical Will* (New York: Dell Publishing, 1969), p. 6.

53 I thank warmly Dominic Bailey, Ella Hermann, Michael Marmarinos, and Eliot Wirshbo for inspiring conversations and/or thoughtful comments on various drafts of this essay.

Chapter 5

Robert Sinnerbrink

SILENCIO:

MULHOLLAND DRIVE AS
CINEMATIC ROMANTICISM

Well, it's all about ideas. And some ideas are painting ideas, and some ideas are cinema ideas. And then the cool thing about cinema is that it embraces time and sounds and, you know, stories and characters, and it goes on and on and on. And it can be like performance. What you're searching for is one of those magic combos of all the elements. And then you get "the whole is greater than the sum of its parts" kinda thing, and then it's worth the trip. I think cinema is like a magnet for people with ideas, and I don't see how they stay away from it for so long.

(David Lynch 2005: 30)

DESPITE ITS REPUTATION as one of the most enigmatic of all David Lynch films, there has been a striking array of critical responses to Mulholland Drive (2001). For many critics, it is a film exploring the complexities of desire and the dissolution of identity, so one best approached from a psychoanalytic or post-structuralist perspective (Cook 2011; McGowan 2007: 194–219; Schaffner 2009). Some have argued that we should undertake the painstaking work of decoding the film's complex and confusing narrative structure (Hayles and Gessler 2004). Others have dismissed this hermeneutic approach, claiming that Lynch's film is a surrealist experiment that defies interpretation, disorienting the viewer by dismantling narrative form in favor of cinematic style (see Chion 1995; Hudson 2004).[1] Martha Nochimson combines elements of both approaches in reading the film not as a divided dream/reality narrative concerning the traumatic relationship between two actresses but as a metafilmic exploration – permeated by Jungian archetypes and cosmic energy metaphysics – of Hollywood's destruction of cinematic creativity, the terrible fate of "the girl" (the female star) expressing "the fate of the industry itself" (Nochimson 2004: 166).

All of these approaches, however disparate and diverse, capture some of the rich texture (a favorite Lynchian term) and complexity of Mulholland Drive. It is a film that defies conventional narrative codes, one that evokes a variety of arresting moods, sensations, and affective responses. Yet despite its opulent narrative and aesthetic mysteries, it is a film that also invites critical attention and philosophical reflection. Indeed, like Sunset Boulevard (Wilder dir., 1950), an important inspiration for Mulholland Drive,[2] it is a metacinematic work that takes as its theme the crisis of cinema itself, depicting the destructive side of the Hollywood "dream factory" in a period of dramatic transition from analogue to digital cinema – a theme elaborated further in Lynch's most recent work, Inland Empire (2006) (Sinnerbrink 2011a: 141–56).

The philosophical reception of Mulholland Drive, moreover, presents a no less intriguing scenario. For some theorists, Lynch's cinema challenges the prevailing rationalism of contemporary film theory. Daniel Frampton, for example, cites Mulholland Drive as a counterexample to the Bordwell/ Carroll cognitivist school of narrative understanding, arguing that cognitive mastery and narrative puzzle-solving are far less important for it than the aesthetic expression of an "affective thinking" revealing a distinctive film world (Frampton 2006: 114). Others take Lynch's films as exemplifying various theoretical approaches, from neo-Lacanian psychoanalytic accounts of fantasy versus desire (Slavoj Žižek, Todd McGowan) to a Deleuzian cinematic philosophy exploring the ways in which sensation, affect, thought, and time can be expressed through movement and time images.[3]

This fascinating array of diverse, even disparate, approaches to the film raises some intriguing questions. Is Lynch's Mulholland Drive a distinctively philosophical film, a case of what Stephen Mulhall (2002/2008) and Thomas Wartenberg (2007) call "film as philosophy" – a film that engages in forms of self-reflection, exploration of philosophical ideas, or complex thought experiments? Or is it an anti-philosophical work, a counterexample to the "film as philosophy" thesis that defies rationalistic analysis, refusing to yield coherent meaning? Taking my lead from the film's enigmatic dualism, I would like to argue that it manages, paradoxically, to be both: not only a brilliant exploration of cinematic/ aesthetic ideas, and meditation on its own cinematic conditions, but a fragmentary neo-romantic work that is expressive and reflective at once. *Mulholland Drive* not only reflects on the history and prospects of cinema in an age of digital transformation, it also provokes an aesthetic experience – fragmentary, imaginative, and poetic – that combines sensation and reflection in aesthetic figures of thought.

By combining an aesthetic of sensation and reflection, *Mulholland Drive* fulfills what the German romantics called for in their philosophy of art: a work that would overcome the divisions between universal and particular, reason and feeling, thereby expressing the utopian image of a unity of thought and imagination, of conscious and unconscious expression.[4] To explore *Mulholland Drive* as a case of cinematic romanticism, I shall analyze one of the most enigmatic passages of the film, the Club Silencio sequence, which showcases Lynch's remarkable combination of visual style, dramatic performance, cognitive disorientation, and cinematic self-reflection. Analyzing the remarkable synthesis of elements in this sequence will give us a better understanding of Lynch's unique style of cinematic thinking. It is a sequence that generates an intensification of our aesthetic experience that serves to provoke thought, both evoking and eluding our desire to master the mystery of *Mulholland Drive*.

Cinematic romanticism

Mulholland Drive is replete with arresting and perplexing image sequences, aesthetic figures, or what Lynch calls "ideas."[5] On the one hand, they serve to provide narrative clues, enigmatic details that promise to yield meaning as the film unfolds; on the other, they appear as stand-alone sequences that set the mood of the film, imbuing the fictional world with its distinctive air of mystery, fascination, and menace. It is this complex ambiguity – combining aesthetic figures with narrative scene-setting, mood with meaning, sense with nonsense – that has arguably generated the plethora of contrary, even opposing interpretations of the film. *Mulholland Drive* generates such responses, I suggest, because it is a neo-romantic work that combines affect and self-reflection, aesthetic abstractions with narrative meaning, in ways that both elicit and thwart narrative interpretation and theoretical analysis.

This observation has been made by other critics, though in a different sense from what I have in mind. Eric G. Wilson (2007), for example, has argued that Lynch's films articulate a "transcendental irony" in the sense conceptualized by the early German romantics – the way literary works can exploit the gap between appearance and reality, play with form and formlessness, use fragments, mix genres, deploy the creative destruction of irony – in order to express the freedom of self-consciousness and to evoke "the Absolute."[6] Taking my cue from the early German romantics, I interpret *Mulholland Drive* as a neo-romantic work that reanimates many of the figures and traits of the romantic work of art. These include a fragmentary style, the use of irony as a way of merging poetic and philosophical discourse, the hybridization of genres and styles, the creative conjunction of conscious and unconscious experience, and the poetic merging of aesthetic figures, rhetorical forms, and conceptual reflection in order to create a work that is poetic and philosophical at once.

The idea that works of art can combine conscious intention and unconscious expression, sensation and imagination, has been essential to romantic aesthetics from the late eighteenth and early nineteenth centuries right up to the present (Bowie 1997; Beiser 2003; Critchley 2004; Nancy and Lacoue-Labarthe 1988). Although often overlooked, the link between cinema and romanticism remains profound and enduring. As Jacques Rancière remarks (2006: 166), the cinema is an art form whose principle, "the unity of conscious thought and unconscious perception," was worked out already 100 years before its advent, namely in the final chapter of F. W. J Schelling's *System of Transcendental Idealism* (1794/1978). With its capacity to combine the mechanical recording of events with the conscious intentionality of the film-maker composing and editing images, cinema, Rancière remarks, "in the double power of the conscious eye of the director and the unconscious eye of the camera, is the perfect embodiment of Schelling and Hegel's argument that the identity of conscious and unconscious is the very principle of art" (2006: 9).[7] It is the ideal art form to express the modern aesthetic regime of art; an egalitarian medium that valorizes subjectivity, confounds the distinction between intentional and mechanical aspects of art, while acknowledging that anything in modern experience is a worthy subject for artistic representation.

Curiously, film scholars (with the exception of Rancière) have not really explored the question of a cinematic romanticism, which is how I would like to approach Lynch's *Mulholland Drive*. It can be viewed as a work of cinematic philosophy, provided we understand philosophy in relation to romanticism, which is to say as an expression of poetic thinking that combines aesthetic and rationalistic, conscious and unconscious, modalities. From this point of view, *Mulholland Drive* is a neo-romantic work that combines cinematic meta-reflection with sensuous immediacy, an affective power to evoke mood and sensation with aesthetic figures expressing abstract thought. Indeed, the mystery of *Mulholland Drive*, we might say, lies in its capacity to express and elicit mood, affect, and aesthetic reflection in a fragmentary work that both invites and resists philosophical interpretation.

Aesthetic ideas

The enigmatic complexity of *Mulholland Drive* continues to provoke philosophical interest and aesthetic fascination. In large part, this is due to Lynch's emphasis on the evocation of mood rather than the development of linear narrative. At the same time, there is no denying the narrative drive in *Mulholland*, the mysteries that the viewer, as much as Betty, is drawn into examining, deciphering, and trying to comprehend.[8] As Lynch often remarks, cinema has the extraordinary capacity to allow stories to be told – or shown – using visual abstractions and aesthetic figures, thereby creating rich textures of mood and meaning, sensation and reflection, that both invite and resist definitive interpretation.[9]

At one level, the film works through what Gilles Deleuze has called, with reference to the painter Francis Bacon, a "logic of sensation": a violent disruption of the representational forms that structure unified subjectivity and instrumental relations with the world (Deleuze 2003). Lynch's work evinces a force specific to the cinematic image that disrupts narrative conventions in order to break through to non-representational levels of sensation and experience (Hainge 2004).[10] As Martha Nochimson remarks (1997: 4–13), Lynch appears to take this view of his own work, describing his films as working through intuitive or "subconscious" awareness (sensuous perception, mood, intuitive understanding) rather than more explicit forms of rational or discursive reflection.[11]

At another level, however, Mulholland Drive engages in a complex reflection on cinematic narrative conventions that renders unstable any straightforward linear interpretation. The result is a work defined by its striking conjunction of sensuous intensity and reflective complexity – a film in which the framework of narrative cinema is undermined even as various narrative and genre conventions are creatively deployed. The resulting conflict between visual, affective dimensions and the demand for narrative coherence arises, I suggest, because narrative is actually *secondary* in Lynch's films to what he calls "ideas." Although Lynch, characteristically, does not explain much what he means (except that ideas are expressions of thought, that they come in fragments, and have an aesthetic consistency that guides his creative film-making practice), I shall define "ideas" here as visual and aural sequences that combine images and sounds liberated from a purely narrative function with those evincing a complex cinematic reflexivity.[12] Such ideas disrupt narrative and representational codes, evoking simultaneously pre-representational sensation and self-conscious reflection upon the nature of film. In a manner recalling Kant's "aesthetic ideas" (1987: 182–86), Lynchian ideas are aesthetic figures that draw together and put into play sensuous intuition and indeterminate reflection; they crystallize aesthetic experience in a manner that discloses indirectly a more complex whole that resists straightforward linguistic or conceptual explication.[13] They are evocative audio-visual sequences, eliciting sensation, affect, and reflection which both provoke and thwart determinate forms of reflection, and thus remain open to infinite interpretation.

We might think, for example, of the opening sequence of Mulholland Drive: the complex foreground and background layering, against a purple background, of multiple 1950s-style dancers in color and "cut-out" silhouette. Against the jitterbug soundtrack the whirling dancers are interrupted by a jerky, white blur of light, revealing the illuminated image of a smiling young woman (Naomi Watts) flanked by adoring older figures (reminiscent of grandparents, though Betty meets them on her flight to LA). The image pulses and sways, being replaced by the smiling face of the young woman, adorned with a brilliant necklace, gazing ecstatically into the distance to rapturous applause. As Martha Nochimson remarks (2004: 167), these surreal and oneiric fantasy images "defy conventional exposition, creating a dreamy, unreal space." Apart from fantasies of stardom, they also foreground the theme of performance, the young woman's success in the jitterbug contest foreshadowing dreams of Hollywood movie success.

All is not well, however, with this cheerful Hollywood fantasy. The brilliant visual sequences interrupting the fantasy soon dissolve into a blurred image of inchoate colors, with the sound of applause drowned out by a muffled "explosion" echoing in the background (one that will recur at the end of the film, with Diane's [Naomi Watts'] apparent suicide by gunshot). This resolves to a subjective point-of-view shot of the carpet, a bed with pink sheets and pillow, accompanied by slow, labored breathing. Is this a dream, a fantasy? Are we experiencing the woman's dying moments? There are certainly darker unconscious forces lurking beneath the surface. This generic, Hollywood fantasy is threatened by darker forces intimating a loss of identity, violence, even death.

It is the conjunction of these dimensions – the disruption of narrative conventions, stylization of subjective experience, and reflexive commentary upon cinematic genre – that gives this particular aesthetic sequence or cinematic idea its aesthetic power. Lynch's strategy is to provoke our desire for narrative coherence, tantalizing us with a desire to know who this young woman is, what her story will be, while at the same time undermining the representational, narrative-driven character of the images, thus leaving ambiguous their narrative significance and opening up a more diffuse experience of mood. This complex aesthetic strategy, as developed throughout the film, both elicits and evades our desire for representational coherence and narrative closure, thereby opening up the properly affective dimensions of mood – of mystery, magic, and menace – that will pervade the film as a whole.

Cinematic dream-work

One of the remarkable features of *Mulholland Drive* is the manner in which it combines image fragments into an oneiric narrative whole. A number of critics have analyzed the way in which the narrative elements of *Mulholland Drive* – notably its dualistic structure, with its mirroring but inverted Betty/Rita and Diane/Camilla storylines – seem to mimic the operations and effects of the Freudian dream-work, with its creation of affectively charged dream images via the condensation and displacement of fragments of waking experience (see Cook 2011; Sinnerbrink 2005; Thomas 2006).

To put it schematically, the Betty/Rita story, comprising the first two-thirds of the film, is composed of fragments taken from the Diane/Camilla story, which comprises the last third, fragments that are transfigured and recomposed – via the processes of condensation and displacement – into a dreamlike fantasy version of events.[14] In the fantasy version, which opens the film, talented, resourceful, and innocent Betty (Naomi Watts), recently arrived in Los Angeles from Deep River, Ontario, to pursue an acting career, promptly rescues the mysterious Rita (Laura Elena Harring) from her car-crash-induced amnesia. She becomes fascinated by this stranger, helping her discover who she is, protecting her from malevolent criminals trying to have her killed, sacrificing her own big break in the movies to help her beautiful but troubled friend (the missed encounter with director Adam Kesher [Justin Theroux] after her stunning audition), until she falls in love with Rita as a mesmerizing specular version of herself (complete with short blonde wig). By contrast, in the Diane/Camilla story, the darker, waking-life version of events, Diane (Naomi Watts) is a depressive actress, struggling to survive on bit parts in Hollywood. She meets and becomes the obsessive lover of the talented Camilla (Laura Elena Harring), who proceeds to take pleasure in humiliating Diane before her lover, talented but arrogant Kesher. This traumatic humiliation prompts Diane to contract a grungy hit man, Joe Messing (Mark Pellegrino), to murder Camilla, an act that prompts a bout of psychotic guilt that ends with her apparent suicide.

Although this dream/reality model captures the essential narrative elements and structure, it does not really account for the film's self-reflexive aspects. Indeed, what is remarkable about *Mulholland Drive* is that this oneiric dream-work process can also be discerned as operating at a *metacinematic* level: taking fragments of cinematic history, canonical films in the Hollywood and European traditions, and submitting fragments of these to the same processes of condensation and displacement, now applied at the level of the history of cinema. This complex operation renders *Mulholland Drive* akin to a collective cinematic dream-work that resonates with the history of Hollywood and European film. It suggests a cinematic palimpsest, evoking fragmentary tropes and images from both traditions, from Wilder's *Sunset Boulevard* (1950) and Hitchcock's *Vertigo* (1958) to Bergman's *Persona* (1966) and Godard's *Le mépris* (1963).[15] Here I would like to focus briefly on one important layer of this cinematic palimpsest or cinematic dream-work, the manner in which *Mulholland Drive* reworks elements of Hitchcock's *Vertigo* as a romanticist/tragic love story of obsessive, self-destructive passion, while at the same time meditating on the history and possibilities of cinema.

There are a number of striking correspondences here, which resonate aesthetically within the cinematic dream-work that is *Mulholland Drive*: for example, the traumatic triggering of Scottie's (James Stewart's) vertigo (after the accidental death of a police colleague), and his obsession with recapturing the illusory figure of the tragically haunted Madeleine Elster (Kim Novak) after her apparent suicide. We might compare this with Rita's trauma-related amnesia (after the "fatal" car accident that, ironically, saved her life), and Betty's growing obsession to resolve the mystery of Rita's murky identity, which results in the shocking discovery of a corpse and Rita remodeling herself in the image of Betty. There are correspondences in appearances: Betty's rather anachronistic hairdo recalls Midge's (Barbara del Geddes') late-1950s blonde bob; Betty's smart gray suit (prominent when she and Rita venture to the Sierra Bonita apartments) is clearly modeled on Madeleine's distinctive gray suit, which Scottie obsessively seeks in order to recreate Judy Barton (Kim Novak) as "Madeleine."

There are correspondences in aesthetic style and mood: the cemetery scene in *Vertigo* where Madeleine contemplates the grave of Carlotta Valdes, shot in muted light with an almost misty/mystical air, is echoed by the courtyard garden scene in *Mulholland* — similarly muted and atmospheric, Betty and Rita arriving at the Sierra Bonita apartments to search for the identity of "Diane Selwyn" by entering her apartment, only to discover a rotting corpse. The tragic love story of Scottie and Madeleine/Judy is based on an illusion that is predicated on the death of the murdered Madeleine, and ends with Scottie's discovery of the truth, liberating him from his vertigo, but also prompting Judy's guilt-induced suicide. The fantasized love story between Betty and Rita, predicated on the murder of the real Camilla, ends with the traumatic revelation of the illusory nature of their love (in the Club Silencio sequence) and the anti-romantic unmasking of their fantasy via the story of Diane and Camilla — a tragic denouement that ends with the revelation of Camilla's murder and Diane's guilt-induced suicide. *Vertigo*'s evocation of a traumatic past that haunts contemporary San Francisco (the tragic romantic story of Carlotta Valdes and her haunting of the melancholy Madeleine, a fatal fantasy that seduces Scottie into erotic obsession followed by devastating depression) is mirrored by *Mulholland Drive*'s evocation of a cinematic history that haunts contemporary Hollywood/Los Angeles: the decaying "dream factory" and fantasmatic setting of Betty/Diane's tragic self-destruction and the oneiric space of the film's metacinematic meditation.

It is not only *Vertigo* that serves as a narrative palimpsest or cinematic dream-work, condensing and displacing elements into a new composition; it is also the topological space of Hollywood (*Sunset Boulevard* displaced into *Mulholland Drive*), to which is added a further layer of cinematic dream-work, namely that relating to the history of European cinema. *Mulholland* reworks, for example, elements from Bergman's *Persona*: the relationship between nurse Alma (Bibi Andersson) and actress Elisabeth Vogler (Liv Ullmann) displaced into that between Betty/Diane and Rita/Camilla, signaled in the well-known shot of their faces, fused in a strangely fractured unity after making love. That these cinematic fragments are reworked within a new context, a work that draws freely upon the history of Hollywood and European cinema while aesthetically transforming these fragments of its cinematic inheritance, only serves to underline the philosophically reflexive status of *Mulholland Drive* as a work of cinematic romanticism. Indeed, from this point of view it is a "film in the condition of philosophy," as Mulhall has put it (2002/2008), reflecting on its own conditions of possibility as well as on the crisis of contemporary Hollywood – its need to recollect its own history, including its relationship with the European tradition, in order to transform itself in the creative transition from the analogue- to the digital-video age.

Club Silencio

Perhaps the most enigmatic sequence in *Mulholland Drive*, the "eye of the duck scene," as Lynch would say (Nochimson 1997: 24–27), is the oneiric performance at the Club Silencio.[16] It is a remarkable example of the film's use of aesthetic ideas, cinematic abstractions, music and performance, in a manner that combines, in good romanticist fashion, affect and reflection, conscious and unconscious processes. It is also an example of what I would call an enveloping or *autonomous mood* sequence in which mood saturates and overflows narrative meaning (Sinnerbrink 2012). Such mood sequences are no longer subordinate to the require-ments of narrative scene-setting or the advancement of plot; rather, they function as independent or quasi-autonomous aesthetic sequences that saturate and exceed the narrative structure. From this point of view, the Club Silencio sequence demonstrates beautifully how cinema can perform philosophy, in a creative sense, by cinematic means: expressing and engaging sensation, affect, and reflection at once, revealing or disclosing hitherto obscured, marginalized, or unfamiliar aspects of our experience of both real and virtual worlds.

After the shocking discovery of a corpse in Diane Selwyn's apartment, along with a large amount of money and a mysterious blue key in Rita's bag, the two women rush back to that apartment where Betty has been staying. The film now reverses the roles between Betty and Rita, with Rita coming to the fore and Betty retreating into the background. Betty helps Rita to cut her hair and don a blonde wig, suggesting that Rita, with her money and key, is connected with the corpse and must therefore change her identity (becoming in effect a reflection of Betty/Diane).[17] At a deeper level, however, it suggests that Diane tacitly acknowledges her own guilt, turning Rita into her double after it becomes clear that Rita has been involved in a murder. Once this transformation/reversal is complete, Betty and Rita consummate their relationship, making passionate love. Their desire for each other now consummated, Rita receives a subconscious message directing them to the mysterious Club Silencio. In a remarkable shot recalling the fusion of faces from *Persona*, Rita emerges from a dreamlike trance, eyes staring into the darkness, chanting "Silencio!" over and over again in an eerie monotone.[18] After a disorienting cab drive, city lights swirling and the visual frame shuddering, they arrive together at the Club Silencio, announced by an evocative blue neon sign.

Like other Lynchian spaces of unconscious aesthetic revelation (*Twin Peaks'* Red Room, *Inland Empire's* movie theater), Club Silencio is a kind of oneiric cabaret theater, its plush interior saturated with deep reds, flashing lights, and plumes of mysterious smoke. A devilish "Magician" called Bondar (Richard Green) – an intriguing director figure – appears on stage and begins his performance, unmasking the dramatic presentation as artful illusion: "*No hay banda!* There is no band, it's all a tape recording, and yet we hear a band . . . it is an illusion." It is the aesthetic illusion of cinematic performance, of the recorded sounds we have been hearing, of the recorded moving images we have been watching; yet these captivating audio-visual illusions also have the aesthetic power to express mood, emotion, and meaning. Cinema is the technologically mediated pursuit of magic by other means, a medium that captures dreams and transfigures experience through beautiful audio-visual illusions. As the Magician demonstrates, the playing of a clarinet, the sound of a muted trumpet, are cinematic illusions conjured up, Prospero-like, by the director's art. We hear a thunderclap, see flashing blue light, hear a muffled explosion (recalling a sound heard in the film's opening jitterbug sequence), disembodied sounds which prompt Betty to shudder uncontrollably, signaling that her fantasy is beginning to decompose (or perhaps marking the moment, in a parallel time frame, when Diane kills herself). His task completed, the Magician fixes us with a sinister glare, is enveloped by thick smoke (recalling Rita's car crash and anticipating Diane's suicide), and slowly disappears into blue light.

The MC for this evening's performance – whom we meet earlier in the film as Cookie (Geno Silva), the flophouse proprietor helping Adam Kesher hide from the Castigliane brothers – now appears on stage, dressed in a sharp red suit. He introduces Rebekah Del Rio, "La Llorana des Los Angeles," who walks on stage in a dazed stupor, as though suffering a traumatic depression, to deliver a poignant Spanish rendition of Roy Orbison's song, "Crying" ("Llorando") (Figure 5.1).[19]

Rebekah Del Rio's performance is the crucial moment in the Club Silencio sequence, which is divided into the Magician's unmasking of

Figure 5.1 Rebekah Del Rio's performance in Club Silencio (*Mulholland Drive*, dir. Lynch, 2001)

what we have been seeing and hearing as cinematic illusion, and Rebekah Del Rio's message to Rita and Betty, revealing the illusory nature of their love – a love predicated on betrayal and death. She takes her place in a line of Lynchian female singers – like the Radiator Lady (Laurel Near) in *Eraserhead* (1977), *Blue Velvet*'s nightclub singer Dorothy Vallens (Isabella Rossellini), and Julee Cruise's poignant and evocative song performances in *Twin Peaks* (1990–91) – whose songs convey unbearable feeling, unconscious trauma, intuitive meaning, performers who seem to have evacuated themselves of any personal subjectivity, becoming instead a pure cinematic expression of desire, sorrow, or loss. The aesthetic power of cinematic performance is revealed as sublime yet illusory; although expressed through images revealing a disembodied voice and a lifeless body, cinema's mechanical recording of action and gesture manifests an aesthetic power to evoke mood and intuitive understanding.

The pain and anguish on the faces of Betty and Rita (Figure 5.2) leave no doubt that they understand the (unconscious) message that their love, indeed Betty/Diane's entire fantasy, is indeed "a sad illusion."[20] As Betty and Rita watch mesmerized, the singer collapses and "dies" on stage. The MC carries her from view, while her song goes on, her disembodied voice reaching an exquisite crescendo: an extraordinary instance of what Michel Chion calls the *acousmêtre*, the disembodied cinematic voice that expresses meaning independently of a character's subjectivity (Chion

Figure 5.2 Rita (Laura Elena Harring) and Betty (Naomi Watts) confront their "sad illusion" (*Mulholland Drive*, dir. Lynch, 2001)

1994). Del Rio's performance and (symbolic) death thus stage aurally and visually the death that Diane has repressed and reinvented as her fantasy love affair with Rita. Betty and Rita apprehend – precisely through the paradoxical revelatory power of illusory cinematic performance – that what we have seen is an illusion, that the love between them is impossible, for Rita, as Camilla, is *already dead*.

Having intuited these meanings, Betty is now prompted to open her bag, in which she finds a strange blue box, the key for which Rita had found in *her* bag earlier in the film. Betty and Rita rush back to the apartment to unlock the blue box and resolve the mystery of Rita's identity. At this point, Diane's fantasy starts to disintegrate. Betty disappears as Rita recovers her bag and puts the blue key in the blue box. As she opens it, the camera disappears into its black core; the box then falls to the floor. We are at the limits of what can be rendered cinematically, a gap or negation of meaning that marks a threshold or portal opening up an alternative reality. Here we encounter the dark secret of Betty/Diane – her murderous desire – and the truth of Rita/Camilla's traumatized identity: her murder as the source of Diane's death wish, her desire for *silencio*. Indeed, the entire narrative thus far is now annihilated (as the fantasy figure of Betty herself is annihilated) in the shot that disappears into the blue box – a cinematic rupture or narrative black hole from which light and meaning cannot return, a figure of negativity that marks a moment of cinematic self-consciousness regarding the limits of film's own powers of representation. At this point, narrative coherence is negated, our desire for the final resolution of the mystery too falling away, just like the blue box – and the mystery of Rita/Camilla's identity – that slips from Rita's grasp.[21]

What to make of this remarkable episode? The Club Silencio sequence, I want to suggest, is a striking instance of cinematic philosophy, synthesizing the aesthetics of preconscious experience with a self-conscious reflection upon cinematic illusion. It is an example of Lynch's cinematic romanticism that combines conscious and unconscious pro-cesses, enveloping moods, and metacinematic reflection. It demonstrates the aesthetic power of cinema, of performance, of the disembodied voice, the liberating ambiguity of cinematic illusion. At the same time, it is the aesthetic medium for the unconscious message that Rita and Betty apprehend through Rebekah Del Rio's stunning performance and startling collapse. The key to the mystery is now revealed: what we have been viewing is a fantasy version of what has *already happened*, Rita/Camilla's death, recorded and transfigured through beautiful cinematic illusion.

This extraordinary fusion of affective, intuitive, and reflective expression – combining visceral affect, aesthetic performance, emotional recognition, and metacinematic reflection – goes well beyond any discrete narrative function or supplementary evocation of mood. The Club Silencio sequence does not simply establish a fictional world or refresh our emotional responsiveness; nor does it serve a primary narrative purpose, delivering us the key to the mystery (which remains as enigmatic and undecidable as before). Rather, it has become a liberated dimension of aesthetic expression, an *autonomous mood* sequence no longer subordinated to narrative ends, one expressive of a multitude of affective and reflective dimensions. In the Club Silencio sequence, mood is no longer a background feature guiding our engagement with characters, but a quasi-independent aesthetic phenomenon that discloses a cinematic world. Mood becomes autonomous, taking on a primary, rather than supporting, role in the aesthetic composition and revelation of a Lynchian world; one that encompasses, in a collective dream-work, fragments from the history of Hollywood movies.

The Club Silencio sequence thus joins the ensemble of Lynchian moments that combine music, mime, song, and performance to communicate narrative meaning by aesthetic means, and thereby comment reflexively on the revelatory powers of cinematic performance. We might think here of the Radiator Lady (Laurel Near) performing "In Heaven" for Henry (Jack Nance) in *Eraserhead* (1977), Dorothy Vallens' melancholy rendition of "Blue Velvet" in the film of the same name (Isabella Rossellini), Julee Cruise's poignant and evocative songs in *Twin Peaks* (1990–91), Agent Cole's (David Lynch's) bizarre "dancing mime" cousin in *Fire Walk with Me* (1992), and Laura Dern's "Battered Woman" performance on screen in *Inland Empire*. Such sequences, recognized as Lynchian signature pieces, aim to create a sense of mystery, revealing darker recesses of meaning in their respective cinematic worlds. They do so by interrupting the narrative flow, blocking the resolution of movement into action, thereby releasing intensive forms of sensation, affect, emotion, and open-ended, indeterminate forms of reflection.[22] We could describe these as "saturated" or autonomous mood sequences that intensify the disclosure of a cinematic world but also heighten its ambiguity and oneiric aspects, thus provoking the viewer to think in response to the aesthetic shock or cognitive disorientation that they experience.

The Lynchian stage/theater space, moreover, also doubles as a figure for the conscious/unconscious mind as well as for the memory of cinema itself. We might call these striking figures – Mulholland Drive's Club Silencio or the film set/Axxon N. theater space of Inland Empire – expressions of the "film as mind" analogy or "filmind," to cite Daniel Frampton (2006).[23] More precisely, these cinematic/oneiric performance spaces stand as figures for the scene of conscious and unconscious thinking; a space in which images, sounds, fragmentary dialogue and action, as well as song and performance, combine to provoke varieties of affect and emotion, moods and reflection. The theater can be a space of aesthetic truth and revelation, as in Mulholland Drive, or a model for the brain/mind or consciousness itself, as in Inland Empire, while evoking and expressing the cinematic presentation of aesthetic ideas. This distinctively cinematic form of revelation is richly rendered in Mulholland Drive, especially in the Club Silencio sequence, which combines the meta-cinematic exposure of the "illusoriness" of the cinematic world, with an emotionally poignant revelation – via song and performance – of the disturbing truth about Betty's/Diane's (fantasized) relationship with Camilla/Rita. These sequences richly deploy Lynchian ideas to communicate the complex relationship between cinema, performance, aesthetic experience, and unconscious intuition. They are autonomous mood sequences staging these ideas as audio-visual sequences that are at once immersive, aesthetic, and self-reflexive.

Lynch's films are replete with such mood sequences that overflow or saturate the narrative situation and thus take on an aesthetic life of their own. Indeed, more rationalist approaches to film narrative (certain cognitivist approaches, for example) tend to overlook or underplay Lynch's aesthetics of mood[24] – an art of cinematic composition involving music, song, sound, color, visual patterning, gesture, narrative, and performance. Such mood sequences play an essential role in Mulholland Drive, a neo-romantic work combining unconscious and conscious processes, pre-reflective sensation and metacinematic reflection. A collective dream-work reprising the history of Hollywood (and European) cinema traditions, it synthesizes these ideas into a richly poetic and philosophically resonant form. It is also a love story, preserving, in silencio, its strange beauty and mystery.

Notes

1   Daniel Coffeen (2003) remarks that "we are not meant to decode the film," since its numinous significance "will be revealed indirectly, in a kind of articulate silence."

2   As Lynch (2005: 273) explains, "There's a shot in *Mulholland Drive* of a street sign that says 'Sunset Boulevard.' I would have loved to put a small piece of the original music in there. And there is a shot of the Paramount Gates, but Paramount won't let you show their logo any more. You can only show the bit of the gate below it. . . . But the car that you see in that shot in *Mulholland Drive* is the actual *Sunset Boulevard* car. I think I found it in Vegas." See Olson (2008: 528–29) for a discussion of *Sunset Boulevard*'s significance for the film.

3   See, for example, the essays in Devlin and Biderman 2011 and in Gleyzon 2010. See Barker 2008 for a reading emphasizing synesthesia. McGowan (2007: 194–219) offers a persuasive Lacanian reading.

4   See Sinnerbrink (2011b) for a discussion of the idea of romantic film-philosophy.

5   As Lynch explains: "Every single thing in the film is based on the ideas. If you could get the whole film as an idea at once, you'd be watching the film from start to finish. But unfortunately ideas come in fragments. Each fragment, though, is full, and it plays in your mind as it comes into you. But it comes in fast, like a spark, and then you start to see it after the light of the spark settles down—there's the idea. . . . The rest of the job is staying true to those ideas. And that seems to be the trick, to translate those ideas to film and stay true to them" (Lynch 2009: 242).

6   For Wilson (2007: 10–25), Lynch's use of transcendental irony points to the underlying metaphysical dimensions of his oeuvre: a Gnostic "non-religious religion" and metaphysics of unified-field consciousness.

7   Schelling writes: "The work of art reflects to us the identity of the conscious and unconscious activities" (1794/1978, 225). See also Garneau and Cisneros 2004.

8   As Lynch remarks, viewers like to play detective, entering a (cinematic) world replete with mystery, danger, and fascination; cinema viewers always try to intuit the meaning of a movie even when it appears unintelligible: ". . . I always say the same thing: I think they [the audience] really know for themselves what it's about. I think that intuition—the detective in us—puts things together in a way that makes sense for us" (Lynch 2005: 287).

9   Lynch elaborates further in an interview: " 'Film can tell and can show abstractions' says Lynch, lighting his last cigarette and running his hands through his hair. 'It is a beautiful language and it is a language that doesn't rely on words. So with sound and picture and timing you can make some beautiful abstractions that other human beings can feel, intuitively, just like they would feel a dream or their subconscious or some abstraction, like going into a room and getting a feeling. That machine kicks in and makes sense

of it. Film is so powerful that way.' . . . 'The beauty of film is that it is a way in which we can communicate the indescribable' " (Lynch 2011, interviewed by Jessica Hundley). See also the remarks in his recent book: "Cinema is a language. It can say things—big abstract things. And I love that about it . . . When I catch an idea for a film, I fall in love with the way cinema can express it. I like a story that holds abstractions, and that's what cinema can do" (Lynch 2006: 17).

10 Hainge argues (2004: 139–40) that there is a strong parallel between Lynch's and Bacon's non-representational "aesthetics of sensation," and that the "bypassing of rationality" in Lynch's films occurs through the "dissolution of narrative."

11 Nochimson (1997: 5) tells the story of looking with Lynch at Pollock's *Blue Poles*: " 'I don't understand this,' I said. 'Yes you do,' Lynch said, 'your eyes are moving.' "

12 Lynch's remarks are worth quoting at length: "Ideas are like fish. If you want to catch little fish, you can stay in the shallow water. But if you want to catch the big fish, you've got to go deeper. Down deep, the fish are more powerful and more pure. They're huge and abstract. And they're very beautiful. I look for a certain kind of fish that is important to me, one that can translate to cinema. . . . An idea is a thought. It's a thought that holds more than you think it does when you receive it. But in that first moment there is a spark. . . . Desire for an idea is like bait. When you're fishing, you have to show patience. You bait your hook, and then you wait. The desire is the bait that pulls those fish in—those ideas. . . . To me, every film, every project, is an experiment. How do you translate this idea? . . . The idea is the whole thing. If you stay true to the idea, it tells you everything you need to know, really. You just keep working to make it look like that idea looked, feel like it felt, sound like it sounded, and be the way it was" (2006: 1, 23, 25, 29, 83).

13 For Kant, an aesthetic idea is "an intuition of the imagination" generating "much thought" but which resists determinate conceptualization, "so that no language can express it completely and allow us to grasp it" (1787/1987: 182).

14 Thomas's fine Freudian reading of the film (2006) details the way in which fragments from the Diane/Camilla story are reworked in the Betty/Rita story according to the logic of the Freudian dream-work.

15 Wilder's *Sunset Boulevard* is explicitly signposted, as it were, while Rita Hayworth as *Gilda* is of course the source of Rita's name during her amnesia. See Laine 2009 for a discussion of the relationship with *Persona*. Godard's *Contempt* [*Le mépris*] is a metacinematic narrative that also ends with the word "Silenzio!" spoken off-screen by the director as the crew prepare to film a scene from the ill-fated Hollywood/European version of Homer's *Odyssey*. Daniel Ross pointed out to me the link to *Le mépris*, a connection also noted by Nieland (2012: 96–97).

16 This is the crucial scene in Lynch's films that provides the vortex of the narrative, a seemingly gratuitous moment that prefigures the end without being a conventional narrative climax. Examples Lynch gives include the "In Dreams" scene at Ben's place in *Blue Velvet* (1984), the dying girl Lula and Sailor discover in a car wreck in *Wild at Heart* (1990), to which I would add Fred's meeting with the "Mystery Man" in *Lost Highway* (1997) and the Club Silencio sequence in *Mulholland Drive*.

17 The resonances with the exchange of identities between actress Elisabeth Vogler and her nurse/confidant Alma in *Persona* are unmistakable.

18 As for Rita's reversion to Spanish, we should note that Rita Hayworth was also a Latina by birth (born Margarita Carmen Cansino), but changed her name in the interests of her Hollywood career (my thanks to Guy Davison for pointing this out). Lynch also mentions how impressed he was by Rebekah Del Rio's Spanish version of Orbison's "Crying," coupled with the "happy accident" that "Laura Harring is half-Spanish, and L.A. is half Spanish, and so Spanish started working its way into the film" (Lynch 2009: 244).

19 Critics have passed over the use of Hispanic performers in the Club Silencio sequence, which evokes the hidden underworld of Hollywood, and suppressed artistic culture of Los Angeles. Thus in Betty's fantasy, Cookie plays a Hispanic underling (the helpful proprietor of the flophouse where Kesher hides), but returns in the Club Silencio sequence to introduce Rebekah Del Rio, "La Llorana of Los Angeles." "La Llorana" ("the weeping woman") refers to an Hispanic folk tale about a woman who is jilted by her husband. In despair she drowns their two children in the river, then after nights of weeping in remorse she drowns herself. Refused entry into the afterlife, she is condemned to search the world for her drowned children, her continuous weeping earning her the name of "La Llorana." Caught between the human and spirit world, it is not difficult to feel the resonance of this tale for Betty and Rita in Club Silencio.

20 The DVD version divides the film into three parts: "She Found Herself the Perfect Mystery"; "A Sad Illusion"; "Love."

21 Lynch (2006: 115) remarks of the box and the key: "I don't have a clue what those are."

22 See Deleuze (1986: 205–15) and (1989: 1–13) on the breakdown of the sensorimotor action schema as revealing new forms of affect, memory, and thought via time images; and Grodal (2009: 145–57) on the blocking of the PECMA (perception, emotion, cognition, and motor action) flow that generates "saturated" emotions and the search for higher-order meanings in art cinema.

23 Frampton (2006: 109) remarks that *Mulholland Drive* is precisely the kind of film that expresses a "filmosophy" or affective thinking that is specific to a particular cinematic world.

24 As Warren Buckland notes (2009: 5), David Bordwell criticizes Lynch on just this score: "And when a film does not conform to classical norms (such

as redundancy), Bordwell regards the director to be amiss: 'If complex storytelling demands high redundancy, Lynch [in *Lost Highway* and *Mulholland Drive*] has been derelict in his duty'."

References

Barker, J. M. (2008) "Out of Sync, Out of Sight: Synaesthesia and Film Spectacle," *Paragraph* 31(2): 236–251.

Beiser F. (2003) *The Romantic Imperative: The Concept of Early German Romanticism*, Cambridge, MA: Harvard University Press.

Bowie, A. (1997) *From Romanticism to Critical Theory: The Philosophy of German Literary Theory*, London: Routledge.

Buckland, W. (2009) "Introduction: Puzzle Plots," in W. Buckland (ed.), *Puzzle Films: Complex Storytelling in Contemporary Cinema*, Malden, MA: Wiley-Blackwell.

Chion, M. (1994) *Audio-Vision: Sound on Screen*, trans. C. Gorbman, foreword by W. Murch, New York: Columbia University Press.

—— (1995) *David Lynch*, trans. T. Selous and R. Julian, London: British Film Institute.

Coffeen, D. (2003) "This Is Cinema: The Pleated Plenitude of the Cinematic Sign in David Lynch's *Mulholland Dr*," *Film-Philosophy* 7(7). (http://www.film-philosophy.com/vol7–2003/n7coffeen) (accessed 19 September 2004).

Cook, R. F. (2011) "Hollywood Narrative and the Play of Fantasy: David Lynch's *Mulholland Drive*," *Quarterly Review of Film and Video* 28: 369–81.

Critchley, S. (2004) *Very Little . . . Almost Nothing: Death, Philosophy, Literature*, 2nd edn, London: Routledge.

Deleuze, G. (1986) *Cinema I: The Movement Image*, trans. H. Tomlinson and B. Habberjam, Minneapolis, MN: University of Minnesota Press.

—— (1989) *Cinema II: The Time-Image*, trans. H. Tomlinson and R. Galatea, Minneapolis, MN: University of Minnesota Press.

—— (2003) *Francis Bacon: The Logic of Sensation*, trans. D. W. Smith, London: Continuum.

Devlin, W. J. and S. Biderman (eds) (2011) *The Philosophy of David Lynch*, Lexington, KY: University of Kentucky Press.

Frampton, D. (2006) *Filmosophy*, London: Wallflower Press.

Garneau, M. and J. Cisneros (2004) "Film's Aesthetic Turn: A Contribution by Jacques Rancière," *SubStance* 33 (issue 103): 108–25.

Gleyzon, F.-X. (ed.) (2010) *David Lynch in Theory*, Prague: Litteraria Pragensia.

Grodal, T. (2009) *Embodied Visions: Evolution, Emotion, Culture, and Film*, Oxford: Oxford University Press.

Hainge, G. (2004) "Weird or Loopy? Specular Spaces, Feedback and Artifice in *Lost Highway*'s Aesthetics of Sensation," in E. Sheen and A. Davison (eds), *The Cinema of David Lynch: American Dreams, Nightmare Visions*, London: Wallflower Press.

Hayles, N. K. and N. Gessler (2004) "The Slipstream of Mixed Reality: Unstable Ontologies and Semiotic Markers in *The Thirteenth Floor*, *Dark City*, and *Mulholland Drive*," *Proceedings of the Modern Language Association* 119(3): 482–99.

Hudson, J. A. (2004) "'No Hay Banda, and Yet We Hear a Band': David Lynch's Reversal of Coherence in *Mulholland Drive*," *Quarterly Review of Film and Video* 56: 18–24.

Kant, I. (1987) *Critique of Judgment*, trans. W. Pluhar, Indianapolis, IN: Hackett.

Laine, T. (2009) "Affective Telepathy, or the Intuition of the Heart: *Persona* with *Mulholland Drive*," *New Review of Film and Television Studies* 7(3): 325–38.

Lynch, D. (2005) *Lynch on Lynch*, rev. edn, ed. C. Rodley, London: Faber & Faber.

—— (2006) *Catching the Big Fish: Meditation, Consciousness, and Creativity*, London: Bobkind/Penguin.

—— (2009) "*Mulholland Drive*, Dreams, and Wrangling with the Hollywood Corral, David Lynch Interview/2001," in *David Lynch: Interviews*, ed. R. A. Barney, Jackson, MI: University Press of Mississippi.

—— (2011) Interview with Jessica Hundley, 9 February 2011. <http://interviewswithicons.wordpress.com/2011/02/09/filmmakerdavid-lynch/> (accessed 15 September 2012).

McGowan, T. (2007) "Navigating *Mulholland Drive*, David Lynch's Panegyric to Hollywood," in *The Impossible David Lynch*, New York: Columbia University Press.

Mulhall, S. (2002/2008) *On Film*, 2nd edn, London: Routledge.

Nancy, J.-L. and P. Lacoue-Labarthe (1988) *The Literary Absolute: The Theory of Literature in German Romanticism*, trans. P. Bernard and C. Lester, Albany, NY: SUNY Press.

Nieland, J. (2012) *David Lynch*, Urbana, IL: University of Illinois Press.

Nochimson, M. P. (1997) *The Passion of David Lynch: Wild at Heart in Hollywood*, Austin, TX: University of Texas Press.

—— (2004) "'All I Need Is the Girl': The Life and Death of Creativity in *Mulholland Drive*," in E. Sheen and A. Davison (eds), *The Cinema of David Lynch: American Dreams, Nightmare Visions*, London: Wallflower Press, 165–81.

Olson, G. M. (2008) *David Lynch: Beautiful Dark*, Lanham, MD: Scarecrow Press.

Rancière, J. (2006) *Film Fables*, trans. E. Batista, Oxford: Berg.

Schaffner, A. (2009) "Fantasmatic Splittings and Destructive Desires: Lynch's *Lost Highway*, *Mulholland Drive*, and *Inland Empire*," *Forum for Modern Language Studies* 45(3): 270–91.

Schelling, F. W. J. (1794/1978) *System of Transcendental Idealism*, trans. M. G. Vater, Charlottesville, VA: University of Virginia Press.

Sinnerbrink, S. (2005) "Cinematic Ideas: On David Lynch's *Mulholland Drive*," *Film-Philosophy* 9(34). <http://www.film-philosophy.com/index.php/fp/article/view/847/759> (accessed 1 July 2005).

—— (2011a) *New Philosophies of Film*, London: Continuum.

—— (2011b) "Re-enfranchising Film: Towards a Romantic Film-Philosophy," in H. Carel and G. Tuck (eds), *New Takes in Film-Philosophy*, Basingstoke: Palgrave Macmillan, pp. 25–47.

—— (2012) "Stimmung: Exploring the Aesthetics of Mood," *Screen* 53(2): 148–63.

Thomas, C. (2006) "'It's No Longer Your Film': Abjection and (the) Mulholland (Death) Drive," *Angelaki* 11(2): 81–98.

Wartenberg, T. E. (2007) *Thinking on Screen: Film as Philosophy*, London: Routledge.

Wilson E. G. (2007) *The Strange World of David Lynch: Transcendental Irony from "Eraserhead" to "Mulholland Dr.,"* London: Continuum.

Chapter 6

Patrick Lee Miller

MONSTROUS MATURITY
ON MULHOLLAND DR.

D AVID LYNCH CLAIMS that this film is easy to understand, but most of its viewers have disagreed. In an interview, he was asked to explain this disagreement, and responded by comparing film – not just this film, but all film – both to music and dreams.[1] Music, he says, is "just an experience," "it is very far away from words," and "there's not an intellectual thing going on." Film "has those same elements of just experience," but whether because of the words spoken by the characters, or some other feature that distinguishes it from music, people falsely believe that their experience of a film can be translated into words. Similarly with dreams: "you tell your friend a dream," Lynch says, "and you can see in the face they don't understand."

This is what happens to Dan who has asked someone to come to Winkie's in order to tell him a recurring nightmare he has about it. We never learn this man's identity – he could be merely a friend, but we may infer that he is a therapist. Even before Dan begins, the look of contempt on the therapist's face anticipates this gap between dream and word. Dan tries to speak, but the failure of his words to communicate his inner feeling is most evident in his effort to describe the ambient time of the dream: "It's not day or night. It's kind of half-night, you know?" But the therapist does not know; nor do we, if we understand knowledge the way philosophers generally do.

Yet an alternate mode of knowledge is possible, according to Lynch: "use your intuition, and then an understanding comes inside you."

Mulholland Drive is "not that difficult to understand," he says, "if you trust your inner feeling." This essay tries to be faithful to that recommendation – recognizing all the while that it is bound to fail, like every argument whose medium is words – by articulating the woolly notion of "intuition" and the vague injunction to "trust your inner feeling." After all, this film evokes many different feelings, and it is by no means clear which we should trust. So although our ultimate goal is to understand it, or at least understand it better, an intermediate goal of this essay is to sketch an alternate mode of knowledge – an alternate epistemology, if you will – that will help us do so.

Important shading in this sketch will follow several lines through teratology, the theory of monsters, a field that has been neglected by most philosophers nowadays, but was earnestly investigated by their Greek predecessors. Aristotle considered monsters to be perversions of the natural order, whereas Plato thought of them as hybrids of conflicting parts.[2] Despite these differences, though, they share central criteria in the definition of a monster: it is a threat to philosophical categories, a disruption of rational thought and stable being, an eruption of the world's irrational becoming. According to Jeffery Jerome Cohen's *Monster Theory*, which is the seminal work of recent teratology, these Platonic–Aristotelian criteria are some of the principal characteristics of a monster more broadly conceived.[3] Others of these characteristics are anticipated by Nietzsche. After developing these two approaches to monstrosity (Plato's and Nietzsche's), along with the rival epistemologies they presuppose, we shall find monstrous the main characters of *Mullholland Drive*. Its deepest lesson, in the end, is that we are monsters too.

Night, half-night, and day

Mullholland Drive is hybrid of a rejected television pilot and a cinematic coda.[4] Lynch called the pilot a body without a head. It would have died, he says in an interview, if he had not found a head to bring it to life. Born from chance, as well as from an imagination worthy of Dr Frankenstein, it was nourished by both as it matured. The result is a film that the director – so usually reticent about the interpretation of his films, and so careful that their DVDs not be divided into chapters – nonetheless divides into three acts. He does not say when each begins or ends, however, so the following divisions are speculative.[5]

The first act emerged from the pilot, whose footage was re-edited once it was incorporated into the feature-length film.[6] Accordingly, we need a name for it that avoids any reference to its genesis. We shall henceforth call it "the night act," the time of dreams. It stretches from the beginning of the film to the scene where Betty and Rita stand before the bathroom mirror in Aunt Ruth's apartment, after they have cut Rita's hair and given her a blonde wig (1:38). The second act stretches from the next scene, when Betty and Rita make love, to the moment when the Cowboy summons Diane Selwyn to wake up (1:57). We shall call this "the half-night act," the twilight of dawn or dusk, midway between dream and reality. The third and final act, "the day act," stretches from her waking to the end of the film. To orient ourselves within the film's bewildering narrative, this tripartite structure will help, but we should also recount the relevant details of each act. We begin, as the film does, with the night.

Of its many narrative threads, foremost is the search for the real identity of Rita. Victim of an attempted hit that was interrupted by a car accident, she flees both its horror and the shadowy syndicate of executives and hit men who pursue her. Descending from the Hollywood hills and crossing Sunset Blvd., she finds refuge in an unlocked Havenhurst apartment. It belongs to Ruth, an old actress who has just left for a shoot in Canada, but it is soon occupied by her niece, Betty. Giddy with excitement – "I just came here from Deep River, Ontario, and now I am in this dream place" – Betty surveys the apartment, beholds herself in a mirror, and then notices Rita showering.[7] Suffering severe amnesia from the car accident, she cannot recall her own name, so when Betty asks nervously after it, Rita responds by looking to a movie poster hanging next to the shower (*Gilda*, starring Rita Hayworth). More precisely, she sees this poster reflected in one mirror, just as we see her reflected in another. Appearing as reflections of separate characters, then, Rita and Betty begin a film-noir search for her real identity. This search will fail, eventually dissolving the distinction between them, not to mention the distinction between reality and its reflected appearances.

They begin with two facts and two memories. The facts: Rita's purse is stuffed with money as well as a shiny blue key. The memories: first the accident's location (Mulholland Dr.), then the name of the waitress who happens to serve them at Winkie's (Diane, which soon evokes "Diane Selwyn"). Equipped with this name and a phone book, their search brings them to the Sierra Bonita apartments. Diane Selwyn no longer lives in the one listed, but the anonymous woman who answers its door has switched apartments with her. A ringing phone distracts her before she can take them to the other. Without a key but under the spell of movie fantasies, Betty cajoles Rita into helping her break in. The technicolor landscape of Hollywood now gives way to a fetid darkness that hides a female corpse. Fleeing in terror the sight of its gray, bloody, and bloated face, their beautiful faces freeze, stagger, and overlap as though the film projector were jammed. The dramatic illusion sustained tenuously throughout the night act thus begins to break down. Indeed, the sharp distinction between its two main characters – Betty the perky, blonde ingénue; Rita the sad, brunette femme fatale – begins rapidly to dissolve. Back safely at Havenhurst, Betty helps Rita cut her dark hair and cover what remains with a blonde wig.[8] The night act ends here, with the two blondes standing side by side before the same bathroom mirror that first showed us Rita adopting her name.

The second act, shot in twilight, opens with their love scene. A tentative goodnight kiss turns passionate, melting the inhibitions that separate their bodies. The consummation is brief, and although we do not see it, we ride on the waves of a musical crescendo worthy of Wagner. The silence of their post-coital sleep is soon interrupted by Rita speaking from the depths of a dream. "Silencio," she intones, adding two other Spanish phrases: "No hay banda" ("There is no band") and "No hay orquesta" ("There is no orchestra"). Waking, and obviously afraid, she insists they go to Club Silencio, where these phrases will be repeated along with others that clarify the lesson: "This is all a tape recording," says the magician who rattles Betty with thunder and flashes of lightning, "and yet we hear a band." Before disappearing in a billow of smoke, he declares: "It is all an illusion." This intellectual comment on the whole film – we the audience also hear a band, so to speak, because we see substantial people who are but flickering images projected through celluloid – is succeeded by its most emotional scene: La Llorona de Los Angeles. While singing "Crying" in Spanish and overwhelming Betty and Rita with grief, she collapses, apparently dead. The emcee carries her off-stage, but her song goes on; it was all a recording. Reaching into her purse for tissues, Betty finds a shiny blue box. She and Rita return in haste to Havenhurst to open it with the key hidden there. When Betty disappears, however, and Rita is left alone to ask "Donde estas?" ("Where are you?"), she opens the box by herself. Looking inside – the camera now adopts her perspective – she descends into its darkness and likewise disappears. This dream is over.

The half-night act concludes with a summons to wake issued by the Cowboy. Although he appears in all three acts, and is the only character to do so, he features in the night's second-most-important narrative thread, which follows the travails of Adam Kesher, director of *The Sylvia North Story*. After Adam rejects the command of the shadowy syndicate to cast Camilla Rhodes as the lead in his movie, he finds himself bankrupt, ousted from his film, and in a corral beneath a flickering light to meet this Cowboy. "There's sometimes a buggy," he informs Adam, teaching him that his ride as a director requires someone else to be the real driver. "Now, you will see me one more time if you do good," he advises before leaving, but "two more times if you do bad." Similarly at the end of the half-night act, as though speaking again on behalf of some omnipotent reality, he addresses a Betty sleeping in the same fetal posture as the Sierra Bonita corpse. "Hey, pretty girl," he says with an uncharacteristic smile, "time to wake up." A second shot of her body shows it as the corpse, and the Cowboy leaves.

Someone then wakes up, thereby beginning the day act, but it is Diane rather than Betty. Both are played by Naomi Watts, a link that tempts us to interpret the first two acts as Diane's dream, the ensuing act as her reality. If any scene were to epitomize this reality, it would be her own account of herself at the posh dinner party off Mulholland Dr., where Adam will apparently announce his engagement to Camilla. After an ironic drum roll from the soundtrack, Diane tells her story to Adam's mother, who seems anxious and bored. "I always wanted to come here," she begins. Back home in Deep River, Ontario, she won a jitterbug contest. "That sort of led to acting," she says, although immediately she feels the need to clarify: "You know, wanting to act." Her aunt was a movie actress who died and left her some money, making it possible for her to come to Hollywood. On the set of *The Sylvia North Story*, she met Camilla, who beat her to the lead she wanted so badly. "Camilla was great in that," says an anonymous man sitting next to her. With a hint of resentment and an awkward pause, Diane replies "Yeah."

Looking fondly toward Camilla, who is seated at the head table next to Adam and speaking Spanish, she resumes. Camilla has since become a star but nonetheless secures small parts in her films for Diane. Hearing this detail, Adam's mother finally shows Diane some sympathy, patting her hand and saying "I see." This gesture seems to make Diane feel ashamed. Looking again toward the head table, this time seeing the host couple laughing together and leaning on one another, her vision blurs – the camera has now adopted her perspective – then refocuses as she stares into her coffee cup. If we credit other scenes in the day act, scenes of frustrated sex and an acrimonious break-up, Diane and Camilla have also been lovers. Toward the end of this dinner party, she sees Camilla flirt openly with another woman. Thus defeated, jilted, and tormented by her beloved, apparently, Diane becomes a monster of grief and jealous rage.

The sound of shattering dishes links the end of this dinner-party scene with the beginning of the next, in Winkie's, where Diane meets a hit man, Joe. All three are shabby counterpoints to the glamour of the dinner party. Their anxious conversation is interrupted first by the dishes and then by the arrival of their perky waitress, Betty, who apologizes, pours coffee, and leaves them alone again. Diane offers Joe a purse with money and a photo-résumé of Camilla. "You sure you want this?" he asks. "More than anything in this world," she replies with a sneer. He promises to signal success with the discreet placement of a blue key. Fixing her eyes with his own, he says "You'll find this where I told you." Distracted for a moment by the glance of a customer waiting to settle his bill at the register – he resembles exactly the night act's Dan – she returns Joe's gaze and asks him: "What's it open?" He answers only with sinister laughter, fading into a dark vision of the vagrant in the alley behind the diner.

Smoke billows behind him as he turns over in his filthy hands a shiny blue box, places it in a crumpled paper bag, and drops it to the ground. All pretense of reality is abandoned when miniature figures dance out of the bag, laughing maniacally. They seem to be the same couple who accompanied Betty upon her dreamy arrival at the Los Angeles airport. As though briefly returning to reality, the next scene shows Diane back in her Sierra Bonita apartment, where she contemplates the blue key on her coffee table. Panning across it and another cup of coffee, we watch her descend into madness. Knocks on her front door herald the miniature couple, who crawl under it. Now grown to full size, as though psychopomps leading her out of the dream place into which they originally accompanied Betty, they pursue her with the same maniacal laughter and fingers outstretched like claws. Running into her bedroom, she collapses onto her bed, reaches for a revolver in the nightstand, and kills herself.

A "Platonic" interpretation

With this articulation of the film into three acts, and the relevant details of its narrative and characters before us, we may indulge for a while a popular interpretation of it that relies on a sharp distinction between appearance and reality, not to mention its cognate distinctions between the images of reflection, dreaming, fantasy, and hallucination, on one hand, and the world outside our imagination, on the other. This popular interpretation, which we shall call "Platonic," will motivate our exploration of the epistemological assumptions we bring to the film, so that once we have distilled the lessons of that philosophical exploration we may return to the film and offer a better interpretation of it, one based on an epistemology closer to the one Lynch expresses in his interviews. Briefly, according to this Platonic interpretation, the day act recounts Diane's failure and fury, and this is the dark, banal, and unifying reality beneath the colorful, adventurous, and disjointed appearances of her dream, which the other two acts project. Although easily stated in brief, this tempting interpretation is much harder to develop in detail. Ultimately, in fact, it proves impossible.

In its crudest form, this interpretation assumes a one-to-one correspondence between characters in the two segments of the film. While the day act gives us real life, according to it, the other acts reflect this reality with dreamy enhancements. The day act shows us Diane in a dingy white bathrobe, for example, whereas the night act's Betty wears a similar one enhanced with bright pink. Although this transposition works to some extent between the Naomi Watts characters – which makes it so tempting a hermeneutic key to unlock the whole film's blue box – it fails to explain the complex associations between others. Both Rita and Camilla, for instance, are played by Laura Elena Harring, but the correspondence between them is looser. In the night act, Rita rides alone in the limousine that makes a surprise stop on Mulholland Dr., but in the day act it is Diane, not Camilla, who does this. If there has been any transposition from reality to dream in this case, then, the real Diane has reflected herself as Rita as well as Betty. Were this not problematic enough, moreover, far more complex associations hold between the minor characters, not to mention between inanimate objects and other aspects of the drama.[9]

If it is to be at all plausible, therefore, this "Platonic" interpretation must permit a fluid relationship between elements of reality and dreams.

Such fluidity can be granted faithfully by recalling Lynch's own comparison between films and dreams, as well as this film's particular discussion of dreams, the one with which we began. Dan dreams of a terrifying monster behind Winkie's. Unfortunately for him, his therapist's contempt for dreams is matched by the naivety of his technique for dealing with them. He tries to pierce Dan's fear by confronting him with its object, with predictably disastrous results. For if Freud is right, dreaming is a compromise between the forbidden "latent content" of our minds and an unconscious agency that protects us from its threat by converting it into the tolerable "manifest content" we experience as the dream. The manifest content thus appears on the surface of the dreamer's mind, while the latent content is a psychic reality below that includes short-term memories from the day before ("day-residue"), long-term memories from as distant as one's earliest childhood, and all the emotions associated with both. The conversion of this latent reality into manifest appearance is far from random, however, because it must satisfy two opposed demands: on one hand, the demand to fulfill the forbidden wishes embedded in the latent content; on the other, the demand to avoid the fear and anxiety that would attend the satisfaction of these wishes in their raw form.

This process of conversion, which Freud calls the "dream-work," uses specific techniques, each analogous to a poetic device. "Displacement" is just metonymy, transposing one element from the latent content into another in the manifest. "Fragmentation" and "condensation" are merely two modes of ambiguity, the first dissolving one element into many, the second fusing multiple elements into one. Substitution of an element's part for its whole is but synecdoche, while exaggeration or diminution of an element are hyperbole and irony respectively. The possibilities are nearly endless, restricted by the urgent need to compromise between the mind's opposed demands of unconscious wish and fear, but in no way restricted by its conscious principles of reason. "Ideas which are contraries," for instance, "are by preference expressed in dreams by one and the same element," thereby flouting the principle of non-contradiction.[10] The principle of sufficient reason fares no better. "A causal relation between two thoughts," Freud writes, "is either left unrepresented or is replaced by a sequence of two pieces of dream of different lengths," although "the representation is often reversed" (OD 6). Dream logic, if it may be called that, is the illogic of poetry.

This is not to say it is random, notice, but only that each association will require its own analysis if we are to understand it, sometimes using one poetic technique, other times using another, but always seeking the same compromise that the mind itself already sought, between wish and fear. Were the final act of Mulholland Drive Diane's reality, and the earlier acts her dream, it would come as no surprise that the association between the elements in the two segments is illogical. Were the life of Diane in the day act to supply the latent content manifest in the earlier acts, furthermore, it should come as no surprise to find there a colorful appearance in which she is displaced onto another character, fragmented into several characters, or fused with someone else into one. And so likewise for the people she meets, especially those about whom she feels strongly, and above all those whom she loves. The transposition from reality to dream does not follow philosophical logic (where contradiction is impossible, and effect must follow cause, future the past) but it does heed the illogic of fantasy (where time and causality are suspended and something can both be and not be itself as well as something else).

Dream characters are thus hybrids, or as Freud calls them, " 'composite structures,' which are creations not unlike the composite animals invented by the folk-imagination" (OD 4). These folk monsters "have already assumed stereotyped shapes in our thought, whereas in dreams fresh composite forms are being perpetually constructed in an inexhaustible variety" (OD 4). That said, dream monsters are of two basic types: good and bad. When the dream-work succeeds, its monstrous creations satisfy the dreamer's wishes without provoking her fears. These are the good ones, and she sleeps on. When the dream-work fails, however, its creations become too scary. These are the bad ones, and she awakes. Freud compares this difference to the two options available to a nightwatchman, "who first carries out his duty by suppressing disturbances so that the townsmen may not be woken up, but afterwards continues to do his duty by himself waking the townsmen up, if the causes of the disturbance seem to him serious and of a kind that he cannot cope with alone" (OD 11).

If Diane is the dreamer, her dream-work successfully suppresses disturbances that manifest as variously as car accidents and murder; she orchestrates all of these monsters into a vibrant and occasionally comic production. But it finally fails when it projects a corpse that shocks by both its rot and its resemblance to herself. With the interruption of her dream-work, her projector jams, and the multifarious characters of its creation begin to resolve themselves into one groggy consciousness. It is only a matter of time – the duration of the half-night act, as it turns out – before her nightwatchman, the Cowboy, arrives to issue the inevitable order: "Time to wake up."

But is Diane the dreamer? To answer this question, and thereby underwrite the "Platonic" interpretation we have now buttressed with Freudian dream theory, we would have first to determine who she really is. That determination proves impossible, however, because it requires us to credit the day act as reality. Hallucination of the miniature old couple makes it incredible, so too does the kiss of the two Camillas at the dinner party that enrages Diane. In this modern setting, the blonde Camilla wears her fifties period costume from the set of *The Sylvia North Story*. Moreover, when she exits the room, she passes the Cowboy, who exits the party. What is a cowboy doing at a gathering of Hollywood glitterati? These are not the only inconsistencies in the narrative of the day act. In the scene on the set of Adam's movie, for example, Diane seethes with jealousy as she watches Camilla being kissed by him. But in the dinner-party scene, when she recounts how she met Camilla on the set of this movie, the anonymous man beside her asks whether its director was Bob Brooker, and she agrees. Or, while Diane stands alone in her drab kitchen, unwashed in her dirty bathrobe, Camilla appears perfectly made-up in her signature red. With tears of desperate joy, Diane exclaims "You've come back!" Immediately, though, her tears turn to sobs that rattle her as she contemplates nothing; nothing, that is, but herself. For the next shot shows her standing where Camilla appeared to be, only contempt now detectable on her face. So which part of this scene was memory, which part fantasy, and which part hallucination?

Once we lose this faith in the reality of this act – and really, this faith cannot be reasonably maintained in the face of so many inconsistencies – it becomes impossible finally to assess the reality of any of its particular scenes. Does Diane have sex with Camilla? Did they ever? Do they break up? Were they ever together? Is there anyone really named Camilla? Most radically, does Diane even exist? This is a peculiar question, whose significance may not even be clear. To answer it, therefore, we now begin a philosophical excursus that aims to provide the background necessary to make its significance clearer. This excursus begins with Plato, then juxtaposes his views – on knowledge, reality, the soul, monsters, maturity, and tragedy – with the rival views of Nietzsche. Only after the contours of this background have been painted in broad strokes can we highlight the precise features of our own interpretation of Lynch's film: Diane does not exist. Properly understood, however, neither do we.

Plato

At the center of Republic, Plato's Socrates distinguishes sharply between knowledge and other cognitive powers. Although many have since rejected details of his distinction, especially the rich ontology he associates with it, most presume its basic tenet: that knowledge requires consistency. Separate powers must deal with separate things, Socrates says, and so for each cognitive power he identifies a different object. Knowledge is infallible, dealing only with what is. Ignorance – deep, deep ignorance – is always wrong, dealing only with what is not. In between these two opposed powers is a third, the fallible power of belief, sometimes right and sometimes wrong. The object with which it deals must likewise lie between the other two. By shortening "what is" to "being" and "what is not" to "not-being," he identifies the object of belief as "what partakes in both being and not being."[11] This contradictory hybrid he elsewhere calls "becoming," the world of change we are all born crediting through our senses (7.519a7–b5). Children do not exhibit the critical reason necessary to eliminate contradiction and think consistently of pure being. Nor do many grow out of this sensual gullibility. Becoming thus remains the basis of "the majority of people's conventional views" (5.479d3–4). But a proper education – culminating in philosophy, which alone pierces hybrid appearances with pure reason – can free us from its seductive power.[12]

The image that illustrates this pedagogy is Plato's most famous, the Cave. "Compare the effect of education and that of the lack of it on our nature," he begins, "to an experience like this" (7.514a1). The Cave is so famous an image that we rarely consider how scary it is. Hearing it from Socrates for the first time, Plato's brother reminds us that "it is a strange image you are describing, and strange prisoners" (7.515a3). As much for us as for the Greeks, who knew caves as the mythical homes of Cyclopes, they were the locus of monsters. Plato makes monstrosity more explicit at the summit of his argument, when he illustrates his psychology by comparing the soul to "Chimaera, Scylla, Cerberus, and the numerous other cases where many different kinds are said to have grown together into one" (9.588c2–5). The bodily appetites are collectively like a "many-headed beast, with a ring of tame and savage animal heads that it can grow and change at will" (9.588c7–9).

Already, therefore, this first part of the soul is a monster: it fuses many heads, of many different types, which change or become through time according to the becoming world reported to them by the senses. Next are the emotions, or at least the emotion of anger, which Socrates compares to a lion as well as a snake. This second part is thus also a hybrid on its own, beholden to the senses and becoming, though corrected by a third part that does not change because it heeds eternal being. Reason, this third part, Plato symbolizes with a homunculus. "Join the three into one so that they somehow grow together naturally," and we have an image of our monstrous humanity (9.588d7–8). The uniform appearance of our skin hides from view the reality of our multiform soul.

Jean-Joseph Goux has shown how Plato built this model of the soul from the materials of Greek mythology.[13] Ancient heroes typically had to earn their status by a journey consummated with the violent killing of a monster: Bellerophon stabbed Chimaera with a lance, Perseus decapitated Medusa with a dagger, and Jason slew from within the Dragon that had swallowed him whole. This "monomyth," Goux argues, depicts an initiation into maturity through which a youth must leave his home and its jealous king, survive fearsome adversity that culminates in the slaying of a monster, and thereby earn a bride of his own else-where.[14] The notable exception to this pattern was Sophocles' Oedipus.[15] He defeated his monster, the Sphinx, not with a violent deed but with a clever word ("Human"). For this innovation, he won not another man's daughter but his own father's wife – in other words, his mother. In Goux's persuasive interpretation of this perversion of the heroic monomyth, Sophocles dramatizes the cost of the Greek enlightenment he witnessed across the span of his life. By trading violent deeds for clever words, the youth never really matures. To marry, this immature man must kill his father, because he has never really left home. So-called oedipal desires are therefore the price to be paid for enlightenment, Greek or otherwise.

Plato takes the next step, according to Goux, putting these new monsters in the soul. Its irrational parts, hydra and lion–snake, shrink from nothing, neither incest nor parricide. By contrast, the rational part, our inner homunculus, seeks only eternal truth, and above all the Good. With this image of the soul, Plato is not thereby condemning us to monstrosity, any more than his cave allegory condemns us to imprisonment. In both cases he admonishes with hope. Perhaps we will be frightened by these images, if not persuaded by the arguments they illustrate, and will then try to resist the temptations presented by the inferior parts of our soul, purge from ourselves the results of their attraction to the appearances of hybrid becoming, and identify finally with pure reason, which is our true nature. This is the promise of his philosophy, an education to help us become who we really are. Maturity, as Plato understands it, defeats monstrosity.

Although most philosophers nowadays reject Platonism, and nearly all would blanch at its invocation of monsters, many nonetheless agree with two of its basic tenets: not only that knowledge requires consistency, but also that maturity requires knowledge. Mulholland Drive challenges this consensus – not with consistent arguments, which would weaken its challenge by hypocrisy, but instead with the sensual images of tragedy, which Plato feared as monstrous.[16] Like all the arts, according to him, tragedy is imitative. Like painting, in particular, it imitates appearances rather than reality, and not just any appearances. The ways of "a wise and selfsame character," someone whose soul is ruled by reason, or the homunculus within, are "neither easy to imitate nor easy to understand when imitated" (10.604e1–3). To most people, the tale of such a character would be boring. With its passionate tales of violence and perversion, by contrast, tragedy imitates the ways of people whose souls are ruled by irrationality, "the part that leads us to recollections of our suffering and to lamentations, and is insatiable for these things" (10.604d8–9). Such tales appeal to most people, whose souls are likewise irrational. Tragedy thus excites "the childish passions that the masses have," by appealing to the monsters that rule their souls (10.608a5). In short, tragedy presents monstrous characters on stage to please the monstrous parts in its audience.

But furthermore, tragedy itself is a monster because it represents the scariest monster of all: becoming. By recalling his chief epistemological distinction – between knowledge, ignorance, and belief – Plato diagnoses the imaginative artist's error as its neglect. Whatever the subject matter, be it shoes, military strategy, or the best way of life, only a fool fails to distinguish between knowledge, ignorance, and imitation. The imitator of human life and character, the tragedian, errs in his making of images because "whatever appears good to the masses, who know nothing – that, it seems, is what he will imitate" (10.602b2–3). Relying in this way on appearances, and especially the unreliable appearances of the ignorant masses, "the maker of an image, the imitator, knows nothing, we say, about what is" (10.601b9–c1). The power of the artist's imagination is not set over what is, then, but instead over what-is-and-what-is-not, being-and-not-being. In other words, his art represents the contradictory hybrid of becoming. Whether or not Plato was right to fear it as such, tragedy – and its modern offspring, cinema – is indeed a hybrid, for this was acknowledged, and even celebrated, by its foremost advocate: Nietzsche.

Nietzsche

Like Plato, Nietzsche understands tragedy by using the distinction between appearance and reality.[17] According to Plato, tragedy presents an appearance of an appearance because it draws its material from the senses, which already report appearances of true reality.[18] With this much Nietzsche, in Birth of Tragedy, agrees. But because his conception of reality inverts Plato's, so too does his valuation of tragedy's doubled appearance. Platonic reality is pure being, free of contradiction, redeeming whoever identifies with reason and thinks of it alone. Nietzschean reality is impure becoming, an eternal contradiction, annihilating whoever is so unfortunate as to behold it naked of all adornment. There are several Greek myths about poor humans who behold a god without adequate preparation. Semele wishes to see her lover, Zeus, in the light of day and is destroyed by the overwhelming sight. Actaeon stumbles upon the chaste huntress-god, Diana, while she is bathing in the company of her nymphs; he is then devoured by his own hounds. In this mythic tradition, Nietzsche describes "the tremendous horror which grips man when he suddenly loses his way among the cognitive forms of the phenomenal world, as the principle of reason in any of its forms appears to break down" (BT 1). The pure being of Plato's cognition, his path to maturity, is in fact a fantasy, one way to cope with an otherwise overwhelming chaos. Reason is reality's clothing, in other words, without which we would all look upon it naked and suffer the punishment of Diana.

One form of the principle of reason is that every effect must have a cause (sufficient reason). Another is that being precludes not-being (non-contradiction). Both receive their first articulation in the poem of Parmenides, whose goddess uses them to lead her initiate onto the sure path of reason and reality, away from the contradictory path of belief.[19] Those who travel the latter are "two-headed," like monsters, "for whom both to be and not to be are judged the same and not the same, and the path of all is backward-turning." These mortals wander through a twilight where "all is full of light and obscure night together." By contrast, should her initiate think only of what is, he will mature into the recognition of his own undying being.

Seeking precedents for his apostasy from her cult of consistency, Nietzsche invokes Heraclitus – here, as elsewhere – by calling contradiction "the father of things."[20] The truth of the world, he believes, is found not through consistent thought but in the transports of Dionysian revelry; not through order, that is, but disorder. "*Excess* revealed itself as the truth," he writes, "and the contradiction, the bliss born of pain spoke out from the heart of nature" (BT 4). Were we somehow able to survive such pain, which in its rawest form destroys the individual, we would be compelled to accept the so-called wisdom of Silenus: that it is best of all never to have been born, and next best to die as soon as possible. But the Greeks who knew this pain nonetheless enjoyed life, so that even their greatest hero preferred to serve a landless man rather than become king over all the breathless dead.[21] The reason they were able to remain aware of the horror of existence without being destroyed by this awareness is that tragedy interposed between it and them a screen of beauty, rendering their life not just tolerable but pleasurable. They were redeemed, in other words, by dreaming, by an aesthetic phenomenon, by the appearance of an appearance.

"Although musical tragedy itself admittedly includes the word," writes Nietzsche, anticipating Lynch in his interview, "it can still at the same time juxtapose the underworld and the birth-place of the word and clarify its development for us from the inside" (BT 21). Neither one without the other would work: words without music would remain lifeless abstractions, disconnected from the reality of becoming; music without words would immerse us in its flow, but deny us the illusion of being that is afforded by our cognition. "Thought and word," he adds, "rescue us from the unbridled outpouring of the unconscious will" (BT 21). Fused together into the hybrid of tragedy, they offer modern Europeans as much as ancient Greeks the redemption of artistic beauty. "Only as an aesthetic phenomenon," Nietzsche famously writes, "are existence and the world justified" (BT 5).

Tragic justification and redemption are available to whole peoples in public spectacles, but also to the individual in the private theater of his dreaming mind. Nietzsche thus reverses Plato's directions to maturity as well as to reality. Rather than waking from our dreams, emerging from darkness into light, and piercing contradictory appearances with pure reasoning about consistent being, we should instead absorb the beauty of these appearances, remain in the twilight between oblivion and consciousness, and exclaim to ourselves joyously: "This is a dream! I want to dream on!" For dreams, like art, "make life possible, worth living" (BT 1). With his attacks on art, dream, and the appearances of becoming, then, Plato's Socrates undermines the foundations of life. Motivated by a "metaphysical madness," he inaugurated "the unshakeable belief that, by following the guiding thread of causality, thought reaches into the deepest abysses of being and is capable not only of knowing but also even of *correcting* being" (BT 15).

Nietzsche sees this madness corrupting Attic tragedy from within, replacing the unconscious forces at work in Aeschylus with the conscious dialectics of Euripides. The result he contemptuously called "aesthetic Socratism," the doctrine that "in order to be beautiful everything must be conscious" (BT 12). In Nietzschean psychology, humans are naturally driven to act and create by unconscious forces, inhibiting themselves from time to time by conscious prohibitions. Socrates, by contrast, acted and created with conscious reason, but was inhibited occasionally by an unconscious voice – his daemonium. He thus inverted the natural order in himself. "Instinct becomes the critic and consciousness the creator," Nietzsche concludes, so that Socrates represents, in his estimation, "a true monstrosity *per defectum*."[22]

If we allow that there are multiple notions of monstrosity – some applicable in some contexts, others in others, but fundamentally divided into the bad and the good, the fearsome and the wholesome – we may agree with Nietzsche that Socrates is a bad monster and tragedy a good one. We may agree, that is, unless we agree with Plato that tragedy is the most fearsome monster of all and Socrates the philosopher its heroic slayer. Beneath this disagreement, however, is a deeper and more important agreement. Whether in Plato's attack or Nietzsche's defense, tragedy presents contradictory becoming, being-and-not-being, appearance and reality mixed together. But whereas Nietzsche sees in this indeterminacy a beauty that could redeem us, Plato sees a seductive monster. Lacking fangs and claws, it appeals to our native desires, and especially our sympathies. That is how it destroys us. "Fear of the monster," observes Cohen, "is really a kind of desire."[23] Rather than resisting this desire as a seduction, according to Nietzsche, we should indulge it as our salvation. From his rival accounts of tragedy and monstrosity, not to mention knowledge and reality, we can now construct our own interpretation of Lynch's film.

A Nietzschean interpretation

Now if any character in *Mulholland Drive* really exists, it is Diane: who else could be the real victim of its illusions, the real dreamer of its dreams? This was the assumption of the "Platonic" interpretation expressed before we elicited the philosophical assumptions that underwrote it. But confidence about real identity and selfhood dissolves in this film as readily as it dissolves within Nietzschean philosophy and its Freudian successor. Nietzsche began with a Platonic distinction between appearance and reality, but eventually subverted it: "The real world – we have done away with it: what world was left? the apparent one, perhaps? . . . But no! with *the real world we have also done away with the apparent one!*"[24] For his part, Freud analyzed the soul into parts, the closest one to a self being *das Ich* – "the ego," or, more accurately, "the I."[25] But whereas the rational self of Platonic psychology was stable, indeed necessary and eternal, every part of the Freudian soul is the product of time and contingency. The Freudian self is produced by ever-changing bodily drives shifting alliances in confrontation with each other and a frustrating world.[26]

Although Freud's systematic tendencies reduced these drives to two (eros and death), he was thereby extending a psychology adopted by Nietzsche from Schopenhauer.[27] While proudly stressing that he read neither, Freud acknowledges "the large extent to which psychoanalysis coincides with the philosophy of Schopenhauer," before describing Nietzsche as "another philosopher whose guesses and intuitions often agree in the most astonishing way with the laborious findings of psycho-analysis."[28] With one short and very intuitive chapter, in fact, Nietzsche anticipates the main notions of Freudian dream theory, not to mention psychoanalytic psychology more generally.[29] "Every moment of our lives sees some of the polyp-arms of our being grow and others of them wither," he writes, evoking Plato's image of the hydra's many heads, "all according to the nutriment which the moment does or does not bear with it." The polyp-arms of our being are our drives, wishes, or appetites; the nutriment they seek is occasionally available in our encounters with reality, but more often supplied by our souls themselves through imagination.

This is especially true of dreams, according to Nietzsche, because "the meaning and value of dreams is precisely to compensate to some extent for the chance absence of 'nourishment' during the day." But it is no less true of waking life, when our desires are just as urgent. "Waking life does not have this freedom of interpretation possessed by the life of dreams," he argues, because the screen on which it projects our daytime fantasies is never so blank as it becomes in the night-time theater of sleep; nevertheless, Nietzsche adds, "there is no essential difference between waking and dreaming." And this is precisely what we should expect from the philosopher who celebrated tragedy, alongside dreams, as the justification of existence. The incoherent and terrifying reality of Dionysus (our latent content) must be transmuted for us by Apollo (into manifest content) if we are to tolerate it. For an individual, the technique of transmutation is dream-work; for the public, tragic art. In every case its projections are merely appearances of an appearance, but our survival requires them, or at least some of them. "I must go on dreaming," Nietzsche writes elsewhere, "lest I perish."[30]

Above all, we need the projection without which we literally lose our minds: the dream of a self (or ego). "We are none of us that which we appear to be in accordance with the states for which we have consciousness and words," Nietzsche writes, because words and consciousness present mere appearances of ineffable unconscious depths where the rational self dissolves into the infinite drives of a mute and irrational body.[31] "The so-called 'ego,'" he concludes, "is thenceforth a fellow worker in the construction of our character and destiny"; just as it comes to be, however, so too can it pass away.[32] Once we experience the dissolution of Diane into incoherent drives – projected as fantasies, always attended by passions, never fully stitched together as a coherent story – then and only then do we understand *Mulholland Drive* with the intuition recommended by Lynch himself. If this intuition could be put into words, the magician at Club Silencio has already done so: "it is all an illusion."

But for whom? Not for Diane, because it persists after her suicide. It is not her dream, then, but ours. As the film flickers to an end, just before we must wake from this public dream and return to the harsh light of an indifferent world, smoke billows around her deathbed. Behind it looms one last time the face of the monstrous vagrant whose appearance always marks a death.[33] His blackened face is now lit by flashes that recall earlier illuminations: the magician's lightning in Silencio, the lamp of the Cowboy's corral, and the headlights on the street sign for Mulholland Dr. itself. Behind the flickering images of this film, then, is a horrible reality to which we all must wake: the ultimate annihilation of self in death.[34]

This is not the reality of Plato: pure being, free of contradiction, redeeming eternally whoever identifies with reason and thinks of it alone. It is the reality of Nietzsche: impure becoming, an eternal contradiction, destroying whoever is so unfortunate as to behold it naked. If this is indeed the nature of things, Plato's injunction to maturity – that we think consistently, strip reality of all its clothing, and grab it for ourselves – is sinister. The consummation of philosophy, which Plato imagines as making love with supreme reality after a long courtship, is in fact a rape.[35] Although his injunction presents itself as a campaign against monsters, Nietzsche unmasks it as the worst sort of monster: the murderous seducer. "Of all errors thus far," he writes later, "the most grievous, protracted, and dangerous has been a dogmatist's error: Plato's invention of pure spirit and of transcendental goodness."[36] Throughout his career he personifies this most dangerous error as Socrates – monstrous always, but especially before death.[37] "Rationality at all costs," he writes near the end of his own career, "life bright, cold, cautious, conscious, instinct-free, instinct-resistant: this itself was just an illness."[38] Lynch seems to agree – not exclusively with words, in the manner of a philosopher, but by superimposing words upon images and music. In the tradition of Aeschylus and Wagner, and against the tradition of Plato and Parmenides, he unmasks the worst sort of monster with the best: tragic drama.

Monsters bad and good

Dan is persuaded to confront the reality behind his fear. He collapses and we feel that within. Betty persuades Rita to seek her real identity. They find only a rotting corpse and we feel that within. The shiny blue key promises to open the shiny blue box, and does. But it terminates a beautiful dream of love and we feel that within. The sum of these and other such "inner feelings" evoked by Mulholland Drive is the intuitive understanding Lynch recommends. This is the ineffable answer to Diane's question to Joe in Winkie's as he holds the blue key before her: "What's it open?" In necessarily hypocritical words: it opens our eyes to naked reality, it wakes us to a world indifferent to our existence, confronting us with the rotting corpse we must all eventually become. Joe answers her more authentically, with wordless, sinister laughter that fades into the mortal vision behind Winkie's. The tempting hermeneutic key to this film — that it presents consistent reality behind the contradictory appearances of a dream — likewise dooms our desire to understand it. For the pernicious monster depicted in these visions is the fantasy of real and pure identity.

We cannot find any such identity because there is none such to be found.[39] There is no being beneath our contradictory appearances. There is only the being-and-not-being of becoming. If we wish to mature in the midst of it, to become who we are, we must try to direct it. But how? This essay has considered two opposed answers to that question. The first was Plato's (enhancing Parmenides'). It enjoined us to look beneath impure appearances to pure reality and understood maturity as moving from the one to the other, as waking from a dream. The second was Nietzsche's (to some extent enhanced by Freud). It rejected as pernicious the fantasy of pure reality beneath impure appearances. Instead it credited only appearances, distinguishing between those that are beautiful, creative, and vital on the one hand, and others that are ugly, destructive, and morbid on the other. This second answer understands maturity not as waking from a dream, but as beautiful dreaming, making good monsters rather than bad. By subverting the distinction between appearance and reality, and by scaring us with a monster at the terminus of the search for real identity, Mulholland Drive assumes something like the second model of maturity.

If Lynch is right, in other words, we should fear the initiation of Parmenides' goddess and avoid her straight path of pure being.

We should instead go two-headed down her proscribed path of being-and-not-being, where "it's kind of half night, you know?" This twilight between dreaming and waking, appearance and reality, illusion and knowledge, is where all of the characters of this film live. It is also where we moviegoers go whenever we knowingly suspend our knowledge that films are illusion. Each one is a waking dream, but few project so well as this one does a harsh reality through the screen of a beautiful appearance, seeming just real enough for us to suspend our disbelief, but not so real that it elicits from us real horror. Mulholland Drive manages not only to enact this contradiction, but to present it to us as a distinctive lesson about our own selves. We are each a dramaturge, it would seem, our selves but characters, and we mature not when we cancel the show to escape the cinema into the noonday sun, but when we dwell in its half-night long enough to project a show that sublimates our longings for beauty and love. Can our creative powers survive the real traumas of an indifferent world while still representing them as beautiful and it as lovable? To do so, we must recognize the necessity of our dreams, our inescapable role as their artists, and our contradictory identity as monsters.[40]

Notes

1 This interview and several others like it are easily available on YouTube. A similar interview can be found in Lynch 2005: 266–94. The comments on intuition and "inner knowing" are on pp. 277–78.
2 Aristotle's teratology can be found in On the Generation of Animals (4.3–6). Plato uses monsters at, among other places, Republic 9.588c.
3 Cohen 1996. For a wider and more recent survey, see Mittman and Dendle 2012.
4 Lynch describes its complex genesis in Lynch 2005: 279–87.
5 Although he does supply clues to the meaning of each in a note on the video sleeve: act 1, "She found herself the perfect mystery"; act 2, "A sad illusion"; act 3, "Love." The first is significantly ambiguous: "she found for herself the perfect mystery" (the identity of Rita), and "she found herself to be the perfect mystery" (as we shall see below).
6 The following website catalogues these many edits: Lost on Mulholland Dr., <www.mulholland-drive.net> (accessed 1 June 2012). Generally, for students of Mulholland Drive, this site is an indispensable mine of facts and theories.

7 In this film, Deep River seems to represent Betty's commonplace innocence, whereas in *Blue Velvet* (1986) the Deep River apartment-building hides that film's most perverse, violent, and gruesome scenes.

8 Lynch uses the motif of a blonde wig—and the alternate identity it creates— in both *Lost Highway* (1996) and *Inland Empire* (2006).

9 Two are especially important. First, Harring's day-act Camilla differs from the Camilla of the night act ("This is the girl"), played by Melissa George, who also plays the anonymous woman of the day act whom Harring's Camilla kisses at the dinner party. How can we understand these nettled associations? Similarly complex is this second set of associations: in the night act, Rita remembers "Diane Selwyn" after seeing the name tag of a Winkie's waitress, played by Melissa Crider, who also plays a nearly identical waitress in the day act, there named Betty, who now serves Diane Selwyn.

10 *On Dreams* 6 (Gay 1995: 159). "Dream-interpretation has laid down the following rule" as it traces the dream's manifest content back to the latent thoughts of the unconscious mind: "if an uncertainty can be resolved into an 'either-or,' we must replace it for purposes of interpretation by an 'and'" (*On Dreams* 4 [Gay 1995: 152]). All subsequent quotations of this treatise will be from the same translation and will be abbreviated in the main text as *OD*, supplemented with a section number.

11 *Republic* 5.478e1–2. Unless otherwise noted, quotations of Plato in this essay are from *Republic*, and particularly the translation of Reeve 2004. Henceforward they will be noted in the main text according to book and line number.

12 Miller 2011 elaborates this story and recounts its contested history in pre-Platonic philosophy.

13 Goux 1993: 140–81 (chs 8 and 9)

14 Ibid.: 5–24 (ch. 1; see also chs 2–4).

15 Ibid.: 82–93 (ch. 5; see also chs 6–7).

16 Plato's critique of tragedy occupies Book 3 of *Republic*, initially, but recurs in a more sophisticated form in Book 10 (595a1–608b3).

17 *Birth of Tragedy* 1. Nietzsche later subverts this distinction, as we shall discuss below (citing *Twilight of the Idols*, "How the Real World Finally Became a Fable"), but he begins his career with a book that depends on it. This shift creates confusion whenever the "Nietzschean" position on the distinction between appearance and reality is mentioned without qualification. Significantly, though, the same confusion should arise with the "Lynchean" position on the same distinction, which is similarly complex, and equally contradictory. Rather than trying to resolve these contradictions, which may not be possible in an even longer treatment, this brief essay aims simply to acknowledge them whenever they affect its argument.

18 For this, the most famous Platonic argument against tragedy, see *Republic* 10.595a1–597e8. For Nietzsche's direct discussion of it, see *Birth of Tragedy* 14. Unless otherwise mentioned, all quotations of Nietzsche are from *Birth*

of *Tragedy*, and particularly the translation of Pearson and Large 2006; references will appear in the main text, abbreviated as BT and supplemented with a section number.

19 See especially B2, B6, B8.9–10 (Curd 1996: 45–47). The next two quotations, from the same translation, are B6.5–9 and B9.3.

20 *Birth of Tragedy* 4 (Pearson and Large 2006: 52), evoking Heraclitus's aphorism B53. His most glowing invocation of Heraclitus comes at the end of his chapter on the Ephesian: "The world forever needs the truth, hence the world forever needs Heraclitus" (*Philosophy in the Tragic Age of the Greeks* 8 [Cowan 1962: 68]).

21 Nietzsche alludes to Homer, *Odyssey* 11.556–58.

22 *Birth of Tragedy* 13 (Pearson and Large 2006: 66). The theme of Socrates as monster recurs later in Nietzsche's career, in *Twilight of the Idols*, specifically "The Problem of Socrates" (3 and 9). He there recounts the following story from Cicero's *Tusculan Disputations* (4.80): "When a foreigner who was an expert on faces came through Athens, he told Socrates to his face that he was a *monstrum* – that he was harbouring all the bad vices and desires. To which Socrates answered simply: 'You know me sir!'" (Pearson and Large 2006: 459).

23 Cohen 1996: 16–20.

24 *Twilight of the Idols* (Pearson and Large 2006: 465).

25 Freudian analysts warn against conflating the notion of selfhood (*das Selbst*), which occurs very rarely in Freud's writing, with *das Ich*. For a sense of their complex relationship (theoretical and textual), see McIntosh 1986.

26 *The Ego and the Id* 2 (Gay 1995: 635–37) and 3 (643–45).

27 On Freud's drives, see *The Ego and the Id* 4 (especially Gay 1995: 645–50); a short note acknowledges the antecedence of Nietzsche on this point (*The Ego and the Id* 2 n. 2 [Gay 1995: 635]), tracing the term "Id" to Nietzsche's use of it for the impersonal forces of the body.

28 *An Autobiographical Study* 5 (Gay 1995: 38).

29 *Daybreak* 119 (Pearson and Large 2006: 198–200). Although Freud's dream theory was less original than he believed, it nevertheless made at least two important contributions to the theory of Schopenhauer–Nietzsche: by (i) articulating the constructive technique of the dreamer's dream-work (that is, its movement from latent to manifest content), he made it possible to reverse directions and practice (ii) the analytic technique of the clinical therapist (that is, the movement from manifest to latent content).

30 *Gay Science* 1.54 (Pearson and Large 2006: 212).

31 *Daybreak* 115 (Pearson and Large 2006: 197).

32 *Daybreak* 115 (Pearson and Large 2006: 198).

33 The other two appearances are: before Diane's hit on Camilla, and before Dan's collapse (presuming, therefore, that he dies).

34 Lights flicker, often because of electrical shorts, in Lynch films as early as *Eraserhead* (1977).

35 *Symposium* 211d2–212b1.
36 *Beyond Good and Evil*, Preface (Pearson and Large 2006: 311–12).
37 Nietzsche's critique of Socrates, especially the dying Socrates, emphasizes both his obsessive rationality and his morbid pessimism. See e.g. *The Gay Science* 4.340, but above all *Twilight of the Idols*, "The Problem of Socrates."
38 *Twilight of the Idols*, "The Problem of Socrates," 11 (Pearson and Large 2006: 461).
39 "All the characters are dealing somewhat with a question of identity," Lynch says in an interview (Lynch 2005: 293). "Like everyone."
40 I would like to thank C. D. C. Reeve, who not only provoked me to think philosophically about this film, but read and helped me revise various versions of this essay. Its thesis was conceived in conversation with Sarah Alison Miller, and was nourished by her work on monstrosity (e.g. Miller 2010).

References

Cohen, J. J. (1996) *Monster Theory*, Minneapolis, MN: University of Minnesota Press.

Cowan, M. (1962) *Philosophy in the Tragic Age of the Greeks*, Chicago, IL: Regnery.

Curd, P. (ed.) (1996) *A Presocratics Reader*, Indianapolis, IN: Hackett.

Freud, S. (1919) "The Uncanny," in *The Standard Edition of the Complete Psychological Works of Sigmund Freud*, vol. 17 (1953–74): *An Infantile Neurosis and Other Works*, ed. J. Strachey, London: Hogarth Press, pp. 217–56.

Gay, P. (1995) *The Freud Reader*, New York: W. W. Norton & Co.

Goux, J.-J. (1993) *Oedipus, Philosopher*, trans. C. Porter, Stanford, CA: Stanford University Press.

Irwin, T. and G. Fine. (eds) (1995) *Aristotle: Selections*, Indianapolis, IN: Hackett.

Kahn, C. (1979) *The Art and Thought of Heraclitus*, New York: Cambridge University Press.

McIntosh, D. (1986) "The Ego and the Self in the Thought of Sigmund Freud," *International Journal of Psychoanalysis* 67: 429–48.

Lynch, D. (2005) *Lynch on Lynch*, ed. C. Rodley, New York: Faber & Faber.

Miller, P. L. (2011) *Becoming God: Pure Reason in Early Greek Philosophy*, New York: Continuum.

Miller, S. A. (2010) *Medieval Monstrosity and the Female Body*, New York: Routledge.

Mittman, A. S. and P. J. Dendle (eds) (2012) *The Ashgate Research Companion to Monsters and the Monstrous*, Burlington, VT: Ashgate.

Pearson, K. A. and D. Large (eds) (2006) *The Nietzsche Reader*, Malden, MA: Blackwell.

Reeve, C. D. C. (2004) *Plato: Republic*, Indianapolis, IN: Hackett.

Index